Ezekiel to Jesus

Ezekiel to Jesus

Son of Man to Suffering Servant

PRESTON KAVANAGH
SIMO PARPOLA

WIPF & STOCK · Eugene, Oregon

EZEKIEL TO JESUS
Son of Man to Suffering Servant

Copyright © 2017 Preston Kavanagh and Simo Parpola. All rights reserved. Except for brief quotations in critical publications or reviews, no part of this book may be reproduced in any manner without prior written permission from the publisher. Write: Permissions, Wipf and Stock Publishers, 199 W. 8th Ave., Suite 3, Eugene, OR 97401.

Wipf & Stock
An Imprint of Wipf and Stock Publishers
199 W. 8th Ave., Suite 3
Eugene, OR 97401

www.wipfandstock.com

PAPERBACK ISBN: 978-1-5326-0976-3
HARDCOVER ISBN: 978-1-5326-0978-7
EBOOK ISBN: 978-1-5326-0977-0

Manufactured in the U.S.A.   JANUARY 16, 2017

Scripture quotations contained herein are from the Revised Standard Version of the Bible, copyright 1952, and from the New Revised Standard Version of the Bible, copyright 1989, each copyrighted by the National Council of Churches of the USA. Used by permission. All rights reserved.

Contents

Chapter 1	Abstract of the Book	1
Chapter 2	New Techniques	7
Chapter 3	The Cyrus Revolt	20
Chapter 4	Ezekiel the Substitute King	26
Chapter 5	Son of Man from Ezekiel Forward	42
Chapter 6	Son of Man in the New Testament	51
Chapter 7	The Assyrian Substitute King Ritual	59
Chapter 8	Letters from Assyrian Scholars	78
Chapter 9	The Babylonian Substitute King Ritual and Christ's Redemptive Death	104
Chapter 10	Jesus the Substitute King	119
Appendix 1	Athbash Letter Exchanges	129
Appendix 2	Eclipses Enthroning Substitute Kings During the Babylonian Exile	130
Appendix 3	Influence upon Son-of-Man Verses in New Testament	132

List of Abbreviations used in Chapters 7–9 | 135
Glossary | 137
Bibliography | 139
Index of Subjects and Modern Authors | 143
Index of Ancient Documents | 147

Chapter 1

Abstract of the Book

AT THE DAWN OF his ministry, Jesus said to a paralytic, "So that you may know that the Son of Man has authority on earth to forgive sins . . . I say to you, stand up, take up your mat and go to your home" (Mark 2:10–11). This is the first of the numerous recorded occasions on which Jesus declared that he was the Son of Man. And though this title lies at the center of Jesus's self-understanding, over two millennia no student of the New Testament has yet proposed an agreed-upon explanation of why Jesus announced himself to be the Son of Man. But we think this book offers such an explanation.

Looking back, we are amazed to have stumbled upon this New Testament find, having spent a full thirty years trying to wring answers from the Hebrew Scriptures about the travails of sixth-century-BCE Jews. (Much of that previous material is included in this book.) But—also looking back—we now realize that the prerequisite for successfully interpreting the Son of Man is learning the identity and fate of the Suffering Servant in the book of Isaiah.[1] Winston Churchill wrote that "Russia is a riddle wrapped in a mystery inside an enigma." The Son-of-Man question is something like Churchill's view of Russia. One must solve a series of enigma-like riddles before arriving at what Jesus had in mind. To explain the mystery of why Jesus chose the Son-of-Man title, we offer the pages that follow, hoping that *Ezekiel to Jesus: Son of Man to Suffering Servant* will trigger a deeper discussion of why Jesus made that choice. To conserve a browser's time and to clarify the argument, here is a short, chapter-by-chapter digest of the entire book.

---

1. This text will rely heavily upon four previous books by the author: *Secrets of the Jewish Exile* (2005), *The Exilic Code* (2009), *The Shaphan Group* (2011), and *Huldah* (2012). The last three were published by Pickwick Publications. Wherever possible, we shall spare readers from excessive noted references to these.

About Chapter 2: New Techniques

Over three decades, your author developed several new approaches to the Hebrew text. Athbash (see Jer 51:41), when modified, proved to be fundamental. Athbash added rotations to facing rows of Hebrew letters so as to offer twenty-two ways to spell any name.[2] (Appendix 1 shows a complete athbash conversion table; this should serve as the basis for all future encoding searches.) Athbash, in turn, brought anagrams (a second technique) into play. These used some or all the letters within Hebrew text words to spell hidden names. Letter sequence was ignored and athbash variations of names invariably employed. For example, "whoring," as frequently used by Ezekiel, contains an anagram for "Huldah." The two were not friends. Our studies found that Huldah was Queen Mother to the exiled King Jehoiachin, and they also brought to light Cyrus. This becomes the first sighting in history of the great Persian commander. Statistically uncontestable Cyrus anagrams in Ezekiel chapter 34 disclose an exilic uprising that went terribly wrong. This will provide one of the keys to solving the New Testament's Son-of-Man mystery.

Encoded spelling is another technique that biblical authors employed. It used one—and only one—letter from consecutive text words to spell a name. A five-letter name would borrow a letter from five Hebrew text words in a row, falling in any sequence. Employing computers, we searched the entire Hebrew Bible for coding of some twenty-five hundred biblical names, both true (the sole original) and athbash (twenty-one variations). Strict probability limits addressed frequency of occurrence by using an extremely conservative acceptance point. (We used a probability of coincidence of not greater than .001.) The net result for the entire testament still exceeded several million encoded spellings. This approach, for example, easily found the identity of Dtr, the long-sought author of Deuteronomy 5–28.

Word Links is a fourth new technique. A Word Link connects two passages that have in their texts the same unique batch of words. This newly modified technique, when tempered by probabilities and enriched by athbash, identified the Suffering Servant of Isa 52:13–15, revealed how King Jehoiachin died (2 Kgs 25:27–30), and attached a name to Second Isaiah (Isa 40–55). Word Links also used an athbash base.

---

2. Kavanagh, *Exilic Code*, 27–33.

About Chapter 3: The Cyrus Revolt

New techniques help to track the movements of Judah's exilic leaders Baruch, Jacob, Ezra, Jozadak, Huldah, Jehoiachin, and Daniel. They served as elders and moved between Judah, Babylon, and Egypt. About 576, they hired young Cyrus to lead a campaign against Jerusalem. The wealth of Huldah and her son Jehoiachin helped to finance the expedition. Although the exiles took and attempted to fortify the city, Nebuchadnezzar returned to the West and put down the rebellion (though one of Israel's neighbors might instead have done that). The probable date of Jerusalem's fall is the spring of 573. Nebuchadnezzar's campaign in Palestine was accompanied by a pogrom against Jews who were already in Babylonia. Ezekiel was captured and imprisoned.

About Chapter 4: Ezekiel the Substitute King

In the ancient Near East, eclipses could lay a death sentence upon rulers, depending upon shading, planetary location, and the like. If portents were bad, the reigning king had only one hundred days to live. To avert their own deaths, Assyrian and Babylonian monarchs enthroned and then killed a substitute. King Jehoiachin was such a case, dying after a 561 lunar eclipse. Earlier, after the solar eclipse of January 5, 569, Nebuchadnezzar selected Ezekiel to be his substitute. Isaiah 52:13–15 is a bulletin announcing that selection.[3] Over one thousand Word Links connect that passage with Ezekiel-related verses. It reported that the prophet, the first Son of Man, had been selected as a substitute king. The flaw in the ritual was that after enthronement the substitute had to voluntarily assume the eclipse's deathly omens, which shifted the death sentence from the true king. The Son of Man refused to assume them and, despite torture, held out until Nebuchadnezzar released the Judeans imprisoned because of the Jerusalem revolt. When read in this context, Isaiah 53, with its tale of redemptive suffering, is now far clearer. So is the matter of how the Suffering Servant extended his days, despite the hundred-day limit on the lives of substitute kings. Chapter 4 concludes by offering dates, authorships, and places of origin for the two Isaiah texts.

---

3. Kavanagh, *Exilic Code*, 118–20.

About Chapter 5: Son of Man from Ezekiel Forward

There is a previously unnoticed line of argument about Ezekiel's goodness and mortality that runs through Scripture and the Apocrypha. The texts usually refer to royalty, celestial bodies, life or death, and the worth or worthlessness of the Son of Man. The trail runs from sixth-century psalms to the Dead Sea Scrolls. Interestingly, Second Isaiah thought that Ezekiel's sacrifice was a good thing but that the Son of Man's days had not been extended to eternal life (see Isa 53:10). Of note are the opinions of the authors of Job and Ecclesiastes. Both strongly objected to the view that Ezekiel was good and lived still. The various views, which bridge the span between Ezekiel and Jesus, are charted within the chapter.

Of prime importance is the identity of the reference to Son of Man, which appeared in Daniel 7. We tentatively conclude that the Daniel author intended to portray a risen Ezekiel, rather than a different substitute from, say, Persian or Seleucid reigns.

About Chapter 6: Son of Man in the New Testament

Experts have been unable to connect the Ezekiel and Jesus models of the Son of Man because they have not discovered the Suffering Servant's identity, nor that the Servant died as a substitute king. Lacking these, many scholars fell back on the Daniel 7 model of an apocalyptic Son of Man. This chapter measures the degree of emphasis of Isaiah 53 and of Daniel 7 on the New Testament's Son-of-Man passages. Mark's gospel leads in the Isaiah 53-Ezekiel type of Jesus. Mark refers to suffering, death, and resurrection in 70 percent of his Son-of-Man verses, while Matthew and Luke are split about fifty-fifty between the influence of Isaiah 53 and of Daniel 7. Surprisingly, the Q Source provides both Matthew and Luke with four Ezekiel-type Son-of-Man sayings that Mark does not have.

Two decades ago, Jesus Seminar scholars rated virtually every Son-of-Man occurrence as having no original connection to Jesus himself. In view of the discoveries in this book, we think it time to reconsider these findings. First, however, a closer look at substitute kings.

ABSTRACT OF THE BOOK

About Chapter 7: The Assyrian Substitute King Ritual

This reprints *Excursus: The Substitute King Ritual* (by Simo Parpola). Citing actual correspondence to seventh-century monarchs Essarhaddon and Assarbanipal, the *Excursus* outlines how these rulers applied substitution in Assyria and in Babylon (Assyria ruled both). Thirty letters to the kings discuss steps to be taken after solar and lunar eclipses. (Eight of sixteen eclipses during their reigns brought a substitute to the throne.) When a *šar pūḫi* and his new queen had been enthroned, the true king assumed the title "farmer" and retired to the sidelines. The substitute next swore to assume the evils that the eclipse had visited upon the true king. The *šar pūḫi* was allowed to reign for up to one hundred days after the eclipse—though never longer. He and his queen were then killed, and given a royal funeral. Sometimes the Assyrians used the same substitute for both thrones, and sometimes they seated only one in Nineveh or Accad (in Babylonia). It depended upon the eclipse.

The *Excursus* concludes with a useful summary of other texts that pertained to substitute kings.

About Chapter 8: Letters from Assyrian Scholars

This chapter gives the text of some two dozen letters from the archives of kings Esarhaddon and Assarbanipal. All pertain to royal substitution. The chilling evidence of human sacrifice accompanied by scrupulously performed rituals is best illustrated here by quoting a single letter (*LAS* 280). It was written to King Esarhaddon in 670 BCE.

> "[Damqî], the son of the bishop of Akka[de], who had ru[led] Assyria, Babylon(ia) [and] all the countries, [di]ed with his queen on the night o[f the . . th day as] a substitute for the king, my lord, [and for the sake of the li]fe of (the prince) Šamaš-šumu-uk[in]. He went to his destiny for their rescue. We prepared the burial chamber. He and his queen have been decorated, treated, displayed, buried (and) wailed over. The burnt-offering has been burnt, all omens have been cancelled, (and) numerous apotropaic rituals, *bīt rimki* (and) *bīt salā' mê* ceremonies, exorcistic rites, *eršaḫunga*-chants (and) scribal recitations have been performed in perfect manner. The king, my lord, should know (this)."

The translations are accompanied by notes and comments. The fact that eclipses were involved brings precision to the BCE dating. The texts are a fitting preface to the concluding chapter.

About Chapter 9: The Babylonian Substitute King Ritual and Christ's Redemptive Death

This chapter contains the translated version of a paper that Professor Parpola presented before the Finnish Oriental Society more than thirty years ago. Very likely it is the first time that any scholar had connected the ancient practice of substitute kingship with the passion of Jesus. The title of the paper carries that message, though all but a few concluding paragraphs deal with sources describing the ritual's use among the Hittites, Assyrians, Babylonians, and Persians, as well as traces of its atoning and sacrificial practice among the Greeks and even the Romans. According to Parpola, Christ's redemptive death was within the framework of substitute practice, except that Jesus took on this role of his own volition.

About Chapter 10: Jesus the Substitute King

Jesus, the preeminent student of Scripture, knew that Ezekiel, the first Son of Man, was the Suffering Servant of Isaiah 53, and that he had died as a substitute king. Taught by Jesus, the synoptic authors and the Q writer also learned these secrets. They framed the synoptic gospels to portray Jesus during his passion to be a later-day substitute king! The parallels between Jesus and Ezekiel are numerous. In the mouths of others, Jesus becomes King of the Jews—over and over and over. Other parallels are a coronation procession (Palm Sunday), last supper, rebels, crown, scepter, soldiers, freed captive, curses, whipping, execution, eclipse, burial in a rich man's tomb, and then resurrection. Jesus, who called himself the Son of Man, emulated Ezekiel, the first Son of Man. Jesus knew that the prophet had become a substitute king, died to redeem others, and then had risen to eternal life. Allowing for different circumstances, Jesus did the same things.

On the whole, today's scholars think that Jesus's Son-of-Man statements were not his own. "The ... Christian community tended to understand the phrase messianically or apocalyptically. The original senses derived from the Hebrew Bible were lost or suppressed," says *The Five Gospels*.[4] *Ezekiel to Jesus* offers the opportunity to change that opinion.

Why not read on?

---

4. Funk and Hoover, *Five Gospels*, 77.

Chapter 2

New Techniques

OVER THREE DECADES, WE found or developed several new approaches to the biblical text. The first was *athbash*, which proved to be fundamental. It is a well-established code within Scripture. The *IDB* defines athbash as "A Hebrew cryptographic scheme in which the letters of the alphabet in reverse were substituted" by using parallel rows of letters.[1] For example, the athbash of Babylon, בבל, is ששך. Jeremiah 51:41 reads, "How Sheshach is taken . . . How Babylon has become an object of horror among the nations!" For the RSV, the meaning of Jer 51:41 was so clear that it simply translated the cipher as "Babylon" and footnoted "Sheshach." The NRSV reversed that, using "Sheshach" and footnoting "Babylon."[2] Jeremiah has a second example of athbash. Two words in Jer 51:1 contain the athbash for "Chaldeans," another term for Babylonians. The Septuagint overrode the cipher and substituted the Greek for "Chaldeans." In doing so, the ancient translator proved that he knew his athbash.

In the athbash cipher, the letters above and the letters below become interchangeable. Following the underlines, the first athbash of יעקב, "Jacob," is מזדש.

יעקב = מזדש

כּ יַ ט חֵ ז וַ ה דָ ג בַּ א

לְ מַ נ ס עַ פ צ קָ ר שֶׁ ת

A biblical author who wanted to encode "Jacob" could use the athbash version, מזדש, as an alternate for יעקב. This gave the writer a greater choice

---

1. Roberts, "Athbash," 306.

2. The NRSV's footnote to Jer 51:41 reads, "*Sheshach* is a cryptogram for *Babel*, 'Babylon.'"

in selecting text words that supported the encoding. But we should not stop at just two versions of Jacob. There are, after all, twenty-two letters in the Hebrew alphabet, and so far we have used but two of them as a first letter—*yod* and *mem*. The way to coax more athbash spellings is rotation of the two lines, much like the rotation of a tractor tread. The first eleven rotations produce eleven new athbash spellings, plus the original true one—twelve in all. To get the final ten spellings, use any one of the athbash words as the reference word and rotate. These rotations of the new reference word yield the final ten athbash spellings. Within Scripture, letters of an athbash spelling may fall in any sequence, provided that they occur within consecutive text words. The ancient writer then had twenty-two versions of Jacob to use in encoding biblical texts. And what works with Jacob works with every name in Hebrew Scripture. We found that multiple-word names such as Jacob-son-of-Isaac were used. Appendix 1 shows all possible athbash interchanges between letters.

Here is anecdotal evidence that someone used rotating athbash to encode the name Jacob in the Second Isaiah text. The first example is from the ninth word of Isa 43:24–25 through the first word of the following verse—seven text words in all. Its translation is, "You have burdened me with your sins, you have wearied me with your iniquities. I, I am He . . ."

1   14   13   12   11   10   9

אנכי בעונתיך הוגעתני בחטאותיך העבדתני אך הרויתני

Within these words, someone concealed numerous coded spellings of four different athbash versions of "Jacob." The first version is נראו. It begins at both words 9 and 12. The next athbash spelling of Jacob is בחכע. It has two rows starting at words 10 and 11. Next, word 10 begins a fresh Jacob version, a single row of עתגה. Finally, two consecutive rows of תוטן commence at words 9 and 10. In summary, these seven text words contain a total of seven coded spellings of four Jacob athbash versions.

Isaiah contains two additional examples. In chapter 54, we find that the prophet packed five different athbash versions of Jacob into his two final verses. Isaiah 41:4–5 offers a change of approach. Here the author coded nine consecutive נראו athbash rows into two adjacent verses. The rows begin at the fourth word of v 4 and end at the second word of v 5. These instances of Jacob coding in the Second Isaiah chapters illustrate the freedom that rotating athbash gave the skillful biblical author.

Anagrams and Cyrus

The second new technique is the *anagram*. Indeed, athbash brought anagrams into play. These used some or all the letters within individual Hebrew text words to spell hidden names. Letter sequence was ignored, and athbash variations of names were regularly employed. For example, "whoring," as frequently used by Ezekiel, contained an anagram for "Huldah." She was Queen Mother to the exiled King Jehoiachin, and anagrams reveal that she also served during the Exile as an elder. In addition, each of twenty-two "elders" text words with Huldah anagrams shelter anagrams for Baruch and for Cyrus. Cyrus! This becomes the first sighting in history of the great Persian commander. Anagrams are simple to derive and would be easy to catalogue and present to others. The first scholars to do so on a comprehensive Scripture-wide basis will perform a great service to the rest of us. Extensive use of anagrams may well open Scripture to learned readers like nothing else that this book discusses.

Examples of athbash anagrams that Jeremiah uses to attack King Jehoiachin follow.

- "Their apostasies [פשעיהם using פשעם, a variation of יוכן] are great" (Jer 5:6)
- "this evil family in all the places where I have driven them [הדחתים using דתהח]" (Jer 8:3)
- "he turns it into gloom and makes it deep darkness [לערפל using עלפר]" (Jer 13:16)
- "I have winnowed them with a winnowing fork in the gates [בשערי using רעשב] of the land" (Jer 15:7)

Exilic authors applied athbash anagrams extensively, and their anagrams often pointed to famous people—favorably or not. A signal example is Cyrus, who in 539 BCE conquered the Babylonian empire. Anagrams reveal the great Persian king to be the Melchizadek of Genesis 14 and Psalm 110. The Genesis excerpt says: "And King Melchizedek [Cyrus anagram] of Salem brought out bread and wine; he was priest of God Most High ... And Abram gave him a tenth of everything. And the king of Sodom said to Abram, 'Give me the persons, but take the goods [Cyrus anagram] for yourself'" (Gen 14:18, 20–21). Cyrus is Melchizedek, he awards Salem (probably Jerusalem) to Abram, Abram pays him, and the king of Sodom (Edom?) proposes a split of booty with Abram.

Melchizedek reappears in Psalm 110. Verses 1–4 contain the Cyrus anagrams: "The LORD says to my lord, 'Sit at my right hand, til I make your enemies your footstool [Cyrus anagram]'... From the womb of the morning [Cyrus anagram] like dew your youth will come to you. The LORD has sworn and will not change his mind, 'You are a priest for ever after the order of Melchiz'edek.'" Lines about corpses, battle, and victory close the psalm. The two Cyrus anagrams give the psalm one of the highest statistical frequencies in the Bible. Considering the two passages together, Cyrus, Abram, and probably Jerusalem are involved, and so are bodies and fighting. The king of Sodom (Edom?) is an ally. This sounds like fighting against intruding neighbors, with Cyrus hired as a mercenary to lead the Israelite army.

Before going further, consider Cyrus anagrams in another passage. The prophet Ezekiel wrote: "Is it not enough for you to feed on the good pasture, that you must tread down with your feet [two Cyrus anagrams] the rest of your pasture; and to drink of clear water, that you must foul the rest with your feet [two Cyrus anagrams]? And must my sheep eat what you have trodden with your feet [two Cyrus anagrams], and drink what you have fouled with your feet [two Cyrus anagrams]?" (Ezek 34:18–19).

This concentration of Cyrus anagrams has no parallel. There are only 999 Cyrus anagrams in all of Hebrew Scripture (which has 305,496 text words). But in Ezekiel chapter 34, which contains only 220 text words, there are eight Cyrus anagrams. The probability that such a concentration is coincidental has sixteen zeroes to the right of the decimal. This is as close to certainty as we can hope to get. Unless others can show that this calculation is erroneous or due to chance, not only do we have a connection between the prophet and the Persian, we have unalterable proof that Ezekiel was using encoded anagrams—a system not yet detected by today's scholars.

The association with Cyrus must have ended badly, so that the Israelites had to live with what the great man had fouled. No talk of Melchizedek now. Whatever happened came after Jerusalem was retaken. And to add force to the anagrams, Ezekiel encoded beneath the text of Ezekiel 34 four spellings of "Cyrus king of Persia" and eleven spellings of "Cyrus king of Anshan."

When could this have been written? There is no reason to attribute Ezekiel 34 to anyone but the prophet, and his final dated prophecy was 573 BCE. Another chapter of this book will conclude that the Babylonians killed Ezekiel in 569. So sometime before 569, the prophet was castigating Cyrus the Great for befouling Judah. Also, Ezekiel and Second Isaiah very likely were contemporaries. Both used anagrams to criticize King Jehoiachin, and both mentioned Cyrus. Ezekiel did it with anagrams and coding, while Second Isaiah specifically named the Persian in Isa 44:28 and Isaiah 45.

Next, consider this famous passage. It summarizes the Judeans' opinion of Cyrus: "My companion stretched out his hand against his friends, he violated his covenant. His speech was smoother than butter [Cyrus anagram], yet war was in his heart; his words were softer than oil, yet they were drawn swords" (Ps 55:21–22).

Cyrus the Great probably was born during the first decade of the sixth century, and we know almost nothing about his early life.[3] He does not emerge on the Near Eastern scene until the middle of the 550s, when—according to the dream of Babylon's King Nabonidus—"Cyrus, king of Anshan, his youthful servant [of Marduk]" would rise against and defeat the Median kingdom.[4] After ruling Anshan in southern Iran for a time, he ascended the Persian throne in 558 BCE, conquered the Medes to Babylonia's north in 550, defeated Lydia about five years later, and in 539 marched unopposed into Babylon. The new king of Babylon then issued a decree allowing Jews to return to Jerusalem to rebuild their temple. Because in the book of Isaiah the Lord calls Cyrus "my shepherd" and "anointed," scholars have reasonably concluded that Second Isaiah made his prophecies closer to 539, when Cyrus took Babylon. This would have meant that Second Isaiah prophesied more toward the Exile's conclusion.

But newer evidence from Scripture offers different information. First, coding in our opening chapter shows that Ezekiel, King Jehoiachin, and Second Isaiah were contemporaries. Ezekiel's last dated prophecy is from 573 and Scripture suggests that Jehoiachin met his death in 561 (2 Kgs 25:27). Next, Ezekiel 34 says—as clearly as text, anagrams, and coding can—that Cyrus king of Anshan befouled Israel. Recall that in Ezekiel 34 the prophet crowded eight Cyrus anagrams into a passage about befouling one's pasture. Psalm 55 added that the Persian harmed his ally and broke his covenant (with speech smoother than butter). This could have happened in the 570s or—less likely—in the 560s, if Ezekiel lived into that decade.[5] Finally, Second Isaiah proclaimed that Cyrus would "build my city and set my exiles free" (Isa 45:13), but apparently the prophet spoke far too soon. The venture that he foresaw appears to have failed utterly. The

---

3. Mallowan, "Cyrus," 7. Mallowan chooses 598 BCE for the birth year of Cyrus.

4. Tadmor, "Nabunaid Inscriptions," 351.

5. To argue against an earlier Cyrus-led campaign, one would have to say that someone other than Ezekiel wrote his chapter 34 and Psalm 55 in, say, the 530s.

historical question is: When did the Israelites came to know Cyrus? The answer is to introduce him in the 570s as the leader of an exilic venture, possibly to retake Jerusalem. But was Cyrus too young to lead such a venture?

Cyrus was a grandson of the Median king, and one can suppose that at an early age Cyrus soldiered in his grandfather's armies. For comparison, at the age of eighteen, Alexander the Great commanded in battle the cavalry wing of the Macedonian army. It is credible, then, that Cyrus in his early twenties could have led troops and abetted revolt in Judah in the 570s. The Genesis 14 account about Melchizedek indicates that Cyrus, the Israelites, and perhaps Edom recaptured Jerusalem. However, disaster must have come next. The revolt apparently was crushed by Nebuchadnezzar, probably with enthusiastic help from Judah's neighbors. The catastrophic consequences were to shape both testaments of Scripture.[6]

Cyrus's intervention in Palestine and the ensuing revolt were years in advance of their proper time. In, say, 573 BCE, the kingdom of Lydia dominated Anatolia to Palestine's north, while the undiminished power of Babylon blocked Cyrus's access to his Persian homeland in the east. Cyrus had not yet even won control over the Medes—it was to be almost twenty years before he could accomplish that. But Cyrus was young and ambitious, and perhaps Second Isaiah convinced the Persian that because God had blessed their enterprise, they could achieve the nearly impossible.

Encoding and Word Links

We have introduced athbash and anagrams. *Encoded spelling* is a third technique which biblical authors employed. Encoded spelling used one—and only one—letter from consecutive text words to spell a name. An encoded five-letter name borrowed a letter from five Hebrew text words in a row. Letters selected could fall in any sequence—sequences that spelled the desired name by using one of twenty-two possible combinations (the original and twenty-one athbash variations). Employing computers, we searched the entire Hebrew Bible for coding of some twenty-five hundred biblical names, both true (the single original) and athbash (the twenty-one variations). Probability theory addressed frequency of occurrence by using an extremely conservative acceptance point, a probability of one in a thousand (.001). The computer retained the rarer spellings and discarded the rest. (That breakpoint is arbitrary. Scholars may wish to vary it to observe the results.)

---

6. For more about this insurrection, see Kavanagh, *Secrets*, 369–70.

The following example shows the fresh power that encoded spelling brings to biblical studies. Chapters 5 through 28 of Deuteronomy constitute the core of the great Dtr's work. He or she is one of the most sought-after identities in Scripture. Measured by statistically significant encoded groups, Dtr's name is Micaiah, son of Gemariah, a young functionary in Judah's court in 604 BCE (Jer 36:11). Micaiah has 140 encoded groups in Deuteronomy 5–28 and is the only person with high-value encoding in every chapter. Close behind is Daniel, with 138 groups. This concentration marks him as either a coauthor or a subject of most Dtr chapters—and certainly identifies him as a flesh-and-blood sixth-century figure. Four other names have one hundred or more encoding groups.[7] This same new practice, encoded wording, also helps establish the context of the Suffering Servant's final days. A future chapter will elaborate.

A fourth new technique that serves well is *Word Links*. Indeed, another chapter will show its use in identifying the Suffering Servant. Still, Word Links is but a modest variation from existing practice, which some experts call intertextuality. The field is well plowed. Scholars have developed categories such as allusion, exegesis, textuality, and interpretation, each with subcategories. Professor Sheri Klouda has written, "The basic term 'intertextuality,' as broadly understood by contemporary literary theorists, embraces all the possible relations that can be established between texts. These relationships can extend from quotations and direct references to indirect echoes and common words."[8] What this book will use is a branch—but just one branch—of intertextuality. It is not intended to supplant other approaches, though the use of probabilities may in itself set Word Links apart.

A Word Link connects two passages that have in their texts the same unique batch of words. That particular batch will appear only in those two passages, and nowhere else in Scripture. A corollary is that the linking words in both passages must be reasonably close together.[9] This writer allowed ten text words as the maximum gap between linked words, though, in practice, batches of linked words were almost always much closer.[10] A

---

7. Kavanagh, *Huldah*, appendix 2, has a complete listing of encoded names, along with the relevant Deuteronomy chapters.

8. Klouda, "Psalm 97 in Isaiah 60 and 62."

9. Another corollary is that identical Hebrew words, such as "serve" and "servant," are interchangeable for linking purposes. Omitting this practice, however, makes almost no difference.

10. Gaps between shared words averaged only 2.9 text words. Lowering maximum

usual Word Link contains six shared words within the length of a biblical verse, which averages thirteen words.

Word Links are easy to use. Adverbs, pronouns, prepositions, common verbs, and well-worn nouns lend themselves admirably to linking. It is the *combination* that matters, not how common or uncommon the words within it are.[11] Those who analyze intertextuality understand that biblical writers often selected their words to accord with other scriptural passages. Word Links takes this one small step forward, recognizing that authors *grouped* those words. The sole measure is vocabulary, so at this stage meaning counts for nothing. And the stress upon vocabulary necessitates that word batches be unique. If duplicates were permitted, a passage could have thousands of meaningless links. Verse divisions were later additions to Scripture, so while analysts may use verses for a first cut to locate Word Links, counted text words are what finally matter.

Another principle is that Word Links ignore composition dates. If two texts share a unique set of words—regardless of when each might have been written—they form a Word Link. Thus, Word Links sidestep a common difficulty in comparing biblical texts. The analyst need not decide which passage preceded the other. He or she is, of course, free to draw such a conclusion, but the linking process in no way depends upon it. However, if authors intentionally fashioned Word Links, how can one explain links between, say, a Second Kings master and a Chronicles text? How can a passage written hundreds of years later throw light upon the earlier one? The answer is that later authors also used Word Links to add dimension and detail to their writing. Their later situation was similar enough to reference an earlier author. Whatever the reason, we can benefit at both ends from the practice—first when we analyze the older text and then as we weigh the younger one.

Word Links handle large numbers of texts at once—hundreds rather than handfuls. In fact, the more texts that are linked with a master passage, the better one's chances are of discovering the full meaning of the master. The preface to the Suffering Servant chapter, Isa 52:13–15, has some eight hundred Word Links—it took that many to identify the Servant of the Lord. Also, the passage that ends the book of Second Kings relates the apparently laudatory release of Jehoiachin from his Babylonian prison. But 468 links

---

gaps from fifteen to ten text words decreases total links by only about 4 percent. The author moved from a fifteen-word limit used in earlier studies to a gap fixed at ten. A gap of nine or even eight would be acceptable.

11. One can form almost four million unique combinations by picking six words from a list of forty.

from that text instead tell a tale of judicial murder. The payoff for the hard work of accumulation comes after sorting linked passages by subject. Aim for several dozen categories and be imaginative. The Jehoiachin passage in Second Kings, for example, finished with 468 links in twenty-three categories—and 92 percent of the links found a home in one of those categories.[12]

Here is a review of Word Links:

- Word Links give additional information about the master passage.
- A link connects two passages that contain the same unique batch of words.
- Linked words inside a text must be reasonably close.
- Vocabulary is the sole basis for selection.
- Only one satellite text may share identical words with the master text.
- Dates of composition should be ignored.
- Hundreds of links are to be expected.
- For analysis, sorting should be done by categories.

Word Links make their own best argument. They work. They give information previously unavailable to students of the Bible, and (as we shall read) help to solve thorny questions such as the identity of the Suffering Servant. There is nothing extreme about these links. They are no more than another category of intertextuality, which most accept. Also, Word Links impose no modern practice upon ancient writers. To the contrary, Word Links—simple to use and easy to find—were fully within the capabilities of those who wrote Hebrew Scripture. To demonstrate, see how a Word Link can reverse the surface meaning of a text. Esther 1:2 says, "In those days when King Ahasuerus sat on his royal throne . . . " However, five Hebrew words from the Esther passage form a Word Link with Jer 36:30. It reads, "He shall have none to sit upon the throne of David, and his dead body shall be cast out to the heat by day and the frost by night." For knowing contemporary readers, that disposed of Ahasuerus.

Another Word Link example comes from a text that very likely yields the name of Second Isaiah, the exilic prophet who makes the short list of history's great religious thinkers. Experts agree that Second Isaiah wrote Isa 49:1–5 and that the passage probably was autobiographical. The opening

---

12. Kavanagh, *Exilic Code*, 42–61, 174–76.

verse reads, "Listen to me, O coastlands, and harken, you peoples from afar. The LORD called me from the womb, from the body of my mother he named my name." That verse contains thirteen Hebrew words, and five of them form a Word Link with the story of the birth of Jacob and Esau (Gen 25:21–26). Since that group occurs together nowhere else in Hebrew Scripture, it is indeed a link. Either Jacob or Esau was the object of Second Isaiah's autobiographical verse—and since Esau is unthinkable, it must have been Jacob. "Jacob" becomes the leading candidate for Second Isaiah's name.

Moreover, our Isaiah 49 passage concludes with "And now the LORD says, who formed me from the womb to be his servant, to bring Jacob back to him . . . " Six of this phrase's ten Hebrew words also lie within the Genesis birth passage, the final words of which are, "Afterward his brother came forth, and his hand [word match] had taken hold of Esau's heel, so his name was called [word match, word match] Jacob [word match]" (Gen 25:26). Word Links between Isaiah 49 and Genesis 25 make a strong case that Second Isaiah's name was Jacob.

The Jerusalem Foray

Using their Egyptian sanctuary, in the early 570s Baruch, Jacob, Ezra, Jozadak, Asaiah, Huldah, and others began to assemble supplies and warriors to retake Jerusalem. These Judean leaders must have realized the consequences that rebellion would bring upon the exiles in Babylon, but nevertheless they went ahead.

Such a venture would have taken money, but the exiles in Egypt had access to it. Anagrams tell us that Huldah and Jehoiachin had grown wealthy through trade, making it probable that they financed the expedition. Ezekiel chapter 27 is ostensibly about Tyre and the wealth that the port amassed by trading. But it is also about the commercial acumen of Huldah and her son Jehoiachin. The chapter is flecked with Huldah anagrams, nearly half of which come from a word that is unique to this text, a word that the RSV translates as "wares." Samples are, "Tarshish trafficked with you because of the abundance of your great wealth; silver, iron, tin, and lead they exchanged for your *wares* [one Huldah and two Jehoiachin anagrams]" (Ezek 27:12). And also, "When your *wares* [one Huldah and two Jehoiachin anagrams] came from the seas, you satisfied many peoples; with your abundant wealth and merchandise you enriched the kings of the earth" (Ezek 27:33). In all, the chapter's text contains seven "wares," a word that Ezekiel fashioned. Obviously, Ezekiel knew his anagrams.[13] First he painstakingly crafted the special word, and then he used it often.

Now, continuing with anagrams, we shall track the Israelites as, starting from Egypt, they launch a campaign to conquer Judah. For information, Asaiah was a war leader and Jozadak and Ezra were sons of Judah's chief priest, which was a hereditary position. The date is about 574 or 573.

Once the army cleared Egypt, arguments arose. "If there is a dispute between men, and they come into court, and the judges decide between them, acquitting the innocent [Jozadak anagram] and condemning the guilty [Asaiah]"; and elsewhere, "... condemning the guilty [Asaiah] by bringing his conduct upon his own head, and vindicating the righteous [Jozadak] by rewarding him according to his righteousness [Cyrus]" (Deut 25:1, 1 Kgs 8:32). Second Chronicles 6:23 has virtually the same wording as First Kings 8 except that it substitutes a Daniel anagram for that of Asaiah. The dispute might have been who was to reign in Jerusalem, as the following suggests: "We have added to all our sins [Jozadak, Jacob anagrams] this evil, to ask for ourselves a king" (1 Sam 12:19). Did Jozadak support Baruch? Proverbs offers this post-mortem: "When the tempest passes [Baruch anagram], the wicked is no more, but the righteous [Jozadak] is established forever" (Prov 10:25). And again, "When the wicked are in authority, transgression increases, but the righteous [Jozadak, Jacob, Ezra anagrams] will look upon their downfall" (Prov 29:16). Jacob (Second Isaiah) and the brothers Ezra and Jozadak seem to have joined in alliance against Baruch.

The Proverbs author had used the same "righteous" spelling before: "The wicked flee when no one pursues, but the righteous [Jozadak, Ezra, Jacob anagrams] are bold as a lion" (Prov 28:1). Another famous phrase that also involved Jozadak was, "Behold, he whose soul is not upright in him shall fail, but the righteous [Jozadak anagram] shall live by his faith" (Hab 2:4).[14] In the same vein, "The ways of the LORD are right [Jozadak, Jacob, Ezra anagrams], and the upright walk in them, but transgressors [Jehoiachin, Koheleth] stumble in them [Jacob, Ezra, Jozadak]" (Hos 14:9, H10). (Koheleth seems to have been another name for Daniel.) As to alignment in these undefined disputes, Jozadak, Jacob, and Ezra always stood

---

13. Ezekiel 27 has sixteen Huldah anagrams—far too many to be coincidental. The probability of coincidence is a miniscule $3.12 \times 10-18$.

14. This Habakkuk phrase was a favorite of the Reformation reformers. Other pro-Jozadak verses are in Pss 86:17, 119:53; Prov 21:26, 29:6; and Isa 45:25.

together with Cyrus, while Asaiah, Jehoiachin, Daniel, Koheleth, and sometimes Baruch were opposed.

Critics of the Jozadak-Ezra-Jacob consortium certainly included the two great prophets Jeremiah and Ezekiel. To them, the military adventure was deathly folly: "Because you trusted in your strongholds and your treasures [Jozadak, Cyrus, Baruch anagrams], you also shall be taken; and Chemosh shall go forth into exile, with his priests [Jacob] and his princes"; "The LORD make you like Zedekiah [Jozadak, Cyrus] and Ahab, whom the king of Babylon roasted in the fire"; and "By ... your understanding [Daniel] you have gotten wealth for yourself, and have gathered gold and silver into your treasuries [Jozadak, Baruch, Cyrus]" (Jer 48:7, 29:22; Ezek 28:4).

Also, the person or persons masquerading as Hosea, Amos, and Micah published the following passages, "You have plowed [Cyrus anagram] iniquity ... Because you have trusted in your chariots and in the multitude of your warriors [Baruch, Cyrus, Jehoiachin], therefore the tumult of war shall arise among your people, and all your fortresses [Jozadak] shall be destroyed"; "The days are coming upon you, when they shall take you away with hooks, even the last [Jozadak, Jacob, Jehoiachin] of you with fishhooks [Baruch]"; and "I will cut off the cities of your land and throw down all your strongholds [Jozadak]" (Hos 10:13, Amos 4:2, Mic 5:11). We can date every one of these dire pronouncements to the later 570s. Clearly, Jozadak, Baruch, Jacob, Jehoiachin, and of course Cyrus were deeply involved in the uprising, and all but Cyrus would pay severe penalties. In the passages quoted below, brackets continue to mark anagrams.

Israel's neighbors were the first to test the newly formed army. An Amorite king summoned his allies: "'Come up to me and help me [Jozadak], and let us smite Gibeon [Daniel]; for it has made peace with Joshua [Asaiah] and with the people of Israel'"; "And the men of Gibeon [Daniel] sent to Joshua [Asaiah] ... saying, 'Do not relax your hand from your servants [Daniel]; come up to us quickly, and save [Asaiah] us, and help us [Jozadak]; for all the kings of the Amorites ... are gathered against us'" (Josh 10:4, 6). Also, "Moab said to the elders of Midian, 'This horde will now lick up all that is round about [Jozadak, Baruch] us ... '" (Num 22:4). Cyrus seemed unrestrained by ancient treaties: "Gibeonites [two Daniel anagrams] were ... of the remnant of the Amorites; although the people of Israel had sworn to spare them, Saul had sought to slay [Cyrus] them ... " (2 Sam 21:2).

Cyrus also helped the Israelites settle old scores. The Samuel of Scripture said, "' ... the LORD has helped [Jozadak] us.' So the Philistines

[Cyrus] were subdued [Jehoiachin] and did not again enter the territory of Israel. And the hand of the LORD was against the Philistines [Daniel] all the days of Samuel" (1 Sam 7:12–13). Gibeon, the Amorites, Moab, Midian, and Philistia make an impressive list for the invading sixth-century Judahites. The main event against the formidable Nebuchadnezzar, however, had yet to be fought.

The Israelites gained possession of Jerusalem. The soundest proof is the previously cited Melchizedek passage in Genesis 14. Verses 16–23 tell how the king of Salem (presumably Cyrus, king of Jerusalem) received homage and tithes from Abram. He, in turn, split up booty with the king of Sodom (probably Edom's king). Those verses contain anagrams for Cyrus (five), Baruch (two), and Ezra and Asaiah (one each). Aside from Ezra, these were Israel's war leaders. Work on the temple apparently began soon after Jerusalem fell: "Then they would give the money that was weighed out into the hands of the workmen who had the oversight [Jozadak, Ezra, Jacob] of the house of the LORD; and they paid it out to the carpenters and the builders who worked on the house of the LORD" (2 Kgs 12:11, H12). Other, though later, passages are similar.[15]

Led by Jozadak, son of the slain high priest, worship seems to have been reinstituted on the site of Solomon's destroyed temple: "The LORD has brought forth our vindication [Jozadak, Baruch, Jehoiachin]; come, let us declare in Zion the work of the LORD our God" (Jer 51:10). But authors in the Minor Prophets objected to overblown religious ceremonies. They pronounced that destruction lay ahead: "Is not the day of the LORD darkness, and not light, and gloom [Asaiah] with no brightness in it? I hate, I despise [Cyrus] your festivals, and I take no delight in your solemn assemblies [Jozadak]"; and "Shall I come before [Cyrus, Baruch] him with burnt offerings, with calves [Jozadak] a year old? Will the LORD be pleased with thousands of rams, with ten thousands of rivers of oil? Shall I give my first-born [Baruch] for my transgression, the fruit of my body for the sin of my soul?" (Amos 5:20–21, Mic 6:6–7). The Jozadak, Baruch, and Cyrus anagrams date these texts to the later 570s.

In the foregoing, we have mixed the new techniques of athbash, anagrams, encoded spellings, and Word Links with a modest foretaste of exilic history. Now let us turn to a fuller explanation of the Cyrus-led revolt.

---

15. Second Chronicles 34:10, 17 are rebuilding verses that contain Jozadak, Ezra, and Jacob anagrams. See also Neh 3:31, 6:16.

Chapter 3

The Cyrus Revolt

THREE THINGS ARE PARAMOUNT among the exilic discoveries that *Ezekiel to Jesus* delivers:

- The appearance of Cyrus in Judah's camp as early as 575 BCE;
- The recapture—and subsequent loss—of Jerusalem in the late 570s; and
- The ritual execution of Jewish leaders by the Babylonians, using substitute kingship.

Athbash, anagrams, encoded spellings, and Word Links are the new techniques that uncovered the first two happenings—the Cyrus and Jerusalem events. This next major discovery is recognition of *substitute kingship*. It stems from the work of Professor Simo Parpola, who coauthors this book. Future chapters will expound these things.

The scholar Rainer Albertz writes that "the exilic period turned into a historical 'black hole' hardly worth recounting and ultimately defying description."[1] Nevertheless, the new methods described previously supply enough for us to move on the New Testament's Son-of-Man question. The "black hole" of information that Albertz characterizes refers to the lack of narratives that might trace what actually happened to the Jews during their exilic years. Instead, they gave us an explosion of Scripture—the Major Prophets, Joshua and Judges, much of Psalms and Proverbs, the Deuteronomistic History, and more. In the main, this volume applies its new techniques to these sources, showing that much of the Exile's history is concealed within the Bible's nonhistorical books.

---

1. Albertz, *Israel in Exile*, 4.

For example, Genesis 24 tells of an unnamed servant who was sent to Mesopotamia by his aged master Abraham to "'go to my country and to my kindred, and take a wife for my son Isaac'" (Gen 24:4). This was to avoid having to select "'a wife for my son from the daughters of the Canaanites, among whom I dwell'" (Gen 24:3). The long chapter relates how the servant encountered the comely Rebekah and convinced her and her father that she should become Isaac's bride. The conclusion was a happy one: Isaac "took Rebekah, and she became his wife; and he loved her" (Gen 24:67). Within the chapter, heavily encoded spellings of Huldah and of her son Jehoiachin reveal that Huldah, the exiled Queen Mother, arranged a marriage for her unmarried son Jehoiachin. She sent to Israel for a bride, and so avoided having to choose a Babylonian wife for the young king. Exiles around the Diaspora would have been keenly interested in a marriage that could carry on the Davidic line, and Genesis 24 was a romanticized account of what actually happened. That essential piece of exilic history was concealed by encoded writing within a patriarchal tale.

Encoded writing and anagrams supply a surprising amount of historical information, with virtually all of it still untapped. We have searched Hebrew Scripture for encodings of only a few exilic names—Jacob, Daniel, Baruch, Huldah, and Jehoiachin among them. Scripture is vast and so is the list of untested names. We urge scholars to begin mapping and start discovering.

After the Babylonians destroyed Jerusalem in 586 BCE, they marched chosen groups of their captives to Babylonia. However, many Judahites remained at large and continued to dwell in Judah. In addition, a sizable number also reached Egypt. More specifically, Ezekiel and Micaiah (with his Deuteronomy scholars) established themselves in Babylonia, while Jeremiah and Baruch were offered the choice of remaining in Judah or trekking to Babylonia. They chose Judah, but shortly thereafter fled to Egypt. Anagrams and encoded spellings tell us that Daniel, Jacob (Second Isaiah), Jehoiachin, and Queen Mother Huldah made their ways first from Babylon to Judah and later to the Jewish colonies in Egypt.[2]

Governance in the Diaspora took the form of councils of elders. The very word "elders" was a favorite for Huldah anagrams—often with anagrams for other notables encoded within that same text word. For example, "He who was over the city [presumably Jerusalem], together with *the elders* [Huldah, Jacob, Baruch, Cyrus, Ezra anagrams] and the guardians, sent to

---

2. Kavanagh, *Huldah*, 10–11 establishes that Huldah was the exiled King Jehoiachin's mother.

Jehu, saying . . . 'we will not make anyone king; do whatever is good in your eyes'" (2 Kgs 10:5). The italicized text words conceal anagrams for five exilic notables. These anagrams may even announce a decision in 573 BCE not to enthrone Jehoiachin until after Jerusalem was secure—if then. Enthroning Jehoiachin in the newly liberated Jerusalem would have been a hot issue. This passage is especially rich because it (a) shows that Queen Mother Huldah in her sixties is a recognized leader of the exiles in Egypt or Judah; (b) places Jacob, Baruch, and Ezra (a contender for the high priesthood and the possible P Source) alongside her; and (c) puts Cyrus, who was then in his twenties, on that governing council of elders. A woman and a young foreign mercenary sitting on the Israelite council of elders! It shows the strains that exile must have put on Judean custom and tradition. On the other hand, people of the stature of Huldah and Cyrus (and Second Isaiah, too) do not appear often in human history.

The period in Egypt was marked by civil strife, as Amasis rebelled against Pharaoh Apries. Josephus writes that a Babylonian invasion of Egypt started five years after the final fall of Jerusalem, or about 581, so Nebuchadnezzar's forays added to the turmoil within Egypt.[3] Presumably, Judean refugees in Egypt would have either remained neutral or fought against Nebuchadnezzar. The Babylonians must have concluded their campaign a year or so later, leaving the Judean settlements in Egypt with a cadre of experienced fighters.

Huldah anagrams appear in "elders" text words over twenty times, which is another example of the Queen Mother's prominence during the Exile. Often, Huldah's opponents skillfully used the "elders" anagram against her. Here they cram two Huldah and Baruch anagrams plus one each for Cyrus and Ezra into six text words. These convert Israelite elders into leaders of Judah's traditional enemies, Moab and Midian: "So the *elders* [Huldah, Cyrus, Baruch anagrams] of Moab and the *elders* [Huldah] of Mid'ian departed *with the fees* [Baruch, Ezra] for divination in their hand . . ." (Num 22:7). Her critics turned Huldah's writings into mere divination. One has to admire the craftsmanship.

Huldah lived into her mid-seventies and retained her extraordinary powers well into old age. The word translated as "old" not surprisingly is from the same Hebrew root as "elders." Here Jeremiah uses both shadings of the root: "Take with you some of *the elders* [Huldah, Cyrus, Ezra anagrams] of the people and some of the *senior* [Huldah, Cyrus] priests" (Jer 19:1).

3. *Ant* 9:7.

Cyrus anagrams accompany the encoding for Huldah in both words, while Huldah herself is said to be among the senior priests—presumably referring to her leadership as a priestess of Asherah.[4] The next text is similar. Earlier in Scripture, when answering Pharaoh's question about who would leave Egypt to worship the Lord, Moses said, "We will go with our young *and our old* [Huldah, Jehoiachin, Baruch, Cyrus]; we will go . . . with our flocks and herds . . ." (Exod 10:9). As one would expect, those who opposed the Jerusalem expedition used Huldah's age against her. In its pithy manner, the book of Job said, "It is not the old that are wise, *nor the aged* [Huldah, Baruch, Ezra, Cyrus anagrams] that understand what is right" (Job 32:9). Isaiah 20:4 uses the identical word (with an identical foursome of anagrams) to paint a verbal picture of captives "both the young *and the old* [Huldah, Baruch, Ezra, Cyrus], naked and barefoot" being led into exile.

Jerusalem Disaster

In 577 or 576, the elders in Egypt reached out to Cyrus, then in his early twenties. The senior leadership must have come to agreement with him, for evidence is strong that he met repeatedly with Huldah and Baruch and with other elders as well. Even though Cyrus was young, by the mid-570s he probably was experienced in war. For comparison, at eighteen, Alexander commanded a wing of his father's army. The Israelite leaders could have made no better choice than Cyrus, who was to become a great statesman and military commander. Thirty-five years after joining the Israelites in Egypt, Cyrus, at the head of his Persians, marched unopposed into Nebuchadnezzar's fabled capital and took down the Babylonian Empire. Cyrus the Great ranks with Alexander, Genghis Kahn, Tamerlane, and Napoleon among history's foremost conquerors.

When the newly constituted army of Israel moved north from Egypt toward Judah, the Israelite leaders must have spent months or even a year in close company with Cyrus. (Imagine being a fly on the tent wall during a discussion between Cyrus the Great and Second Isaiah!) This gives fuller context to the amazing statement in Isa 45:1, "Thus says the LORD to his anointed, to Cyrus, whose right hand I have grasped . . ." It is likely that Jacob and the other leaders had anointed the Persian in the name of the Lord.

Isaiah 22, describing a battle at Jerusalem, mentions chariots and horsemen from Elam, indicating that Cyrus brought with him a contingent

---

4. For Huldah's position in the Asherah, see Kavanagh, *Huldah*, 49–50.

of Persian mercenaries. The book of Joshua describes the campaign.[5] (The Babylonians did not garrison their conquests, and so were not on the scene.) The siege of Jericho was noteworthy. The Israelite army, camped before the city, needed a new commander, and Asaiah was the choice. To relate the tale, the writer selected an appropriate Asaiah anagram, which was "Joshua." Because an athbash of Asaiah's name contains the letters spelling "Joshua," it is not unlikely that Asaiah commanded when the returning Judeans besieged Jericho. Here is the text:

> When *Joshua* [Asaiah anagram] was by Jericho, he lifted up his eyes and looked, and behold, a man stood before him with his drawn sword in his hand; and *Joshua* [Asaiah] went to him and said to him, "Are you for us or for our adversaries?" And he said, "No; but as commander of the army of the LORD I have now come." And *Joshua* [Asaiah] fell on his face to the earth, and worshipped, and said to him, "What does my LORD bid his servant?" And the commander of the Lord's army said to *Joshua* [Asaiah], "Put off your shoes from your feet; for the place where you stand is holy." And *Joshua* [Asaiah] did so. (Josh 5:13–15)

The ensuing chapters of Scripture are likewise filled with Asaiah anagrams, which on occasion accompany those for Huldah, Cyrus, Daniel, and Baruch. This is an account of a sixth-century taking, encoded within the story of a far-earlier conquest of the Promised Land. Perhaps the pages circulated quickly across the width of the Diaspora, a sort of war reporting. Analysts agree that it is a Deuteronomistic composition.[6]

After the Jericho victory, the Israelites marched on ruined Jerusalem and then hurriedly attempted to reconstruct the city's defenses. The date of the recapture was about 574. At the same time, the elders and others worked at establishing the new community and dividing the land among those who had trekked from Egypt and shared in the fighting. But disaster followed.

April 28, 573 BCE is the last exact date that the book of Ezekiel records. The chapter so dated, Ezekiel 40 launches the prophet's blueprint for restoration of the temple, and it also opens with a Huldah anagram (which may indicate the name of his editor): "In the twenty-fifth year of our exile, at the beginning of the year, on the *tenth* [Huldah anagram] day of the month . . . " (Ezek 40:1). We think that this dates Jerusalem's recapture by enemies—either by Nebuchadnezzar or by an alliance of neighbors. Appropriately, Ezekiel

---

5. Kavanagh, *Huldah*, 53.
6. Boling, "Joshua," 1007.

laid out the dimensions of the new city in a text dated on the day, month, and year of the city's destruction. The long (and not engaging) chapter is crammed with Jehoiachin coded spellings. Given the context, the encodings indicate that King Jehoiachin was captured at the Jerusalem site. Daniel, Baruch, and Asaiah probably also were taken, while Huldah and Cyrus escaped. All the high hopes that Second Isaiah had raised were dashed. The other Judahite leaders had been captured, were running for their lives, or had been slain—and the slaughter was considerable. It was the nadir of the Exile.

A poignant poem, probably by Huldah, may mourn that disaster. Ostensibly, it is David's death-dirge over Saul; instead, it might lament one of the outcomes of Jerusalem's second fall—perhaps the capture of King Jehoiachin. The author relies heavily upon anagrams, which are shown in brackets.

> *Thy glory* [Jacob], O Israel, is slain upon your high places! How are the *mighty* [Huldah, Jehoiachin] fallen! Tell it not in Gath, *publish* [Huldah] it not in the streets of Ashkelon; lest the daughters of the Philistines rejoice, lest the daughters of the *uncircumcised* [Huldah] exult. Ye mountains of Gilboa, let there be no dew or rain upon you, nor up surging of the deep! For there the shield of the *mighty* [Huldah, Jehoiachin] was defiled, the shield of Saul, not *anointed* [messiah] with oil. From the blood of the slain, from the fat of the *mighty* [Huldah, Jehoiachin], the bow of Jonathan turned not back, and the sword of Saul returned not empty . . . How are the *mighty* [Huldah, Jehoiachin] fallen, and the weapons of war perished! (2 Sam 1:19–22, 27)

When the uprising occurred, a substantial number of Judeans had been exiled in Babylonia for a quarter century. They must have been appalled to learn of the revolt in the west, and they paid as dearly for it as their countrymen at Jerusalem. A pogrom against the exiles in Babylon would have quickly followed as authorities harvested both lives and possessions. Daniel, Huldah, and Jehoiachin had departed from Babylonia years earlier to rally their countrymen in Egypt. This left Ezekiel, who certainly opposed the revolt, as the leading Judean citizen in the east. His last writing was dated in the spring of 573, so imprisonment must have followed shortly thereafter.

Virtually all of this exilic history comes to light because of the newly discovered athbash, anagram, encoded writing, and Word Link applications. For this writer, at least, that fresh knowledge becomes a necessary prologue to determining why Jesus used the title Son of Man. Knowing Ezekiel's fate becomes a vital part of the bridge between the Exile's tragedy and the persona of Jesus.

Chapter 4

Ezekiel the Substitute King

King Nebuchadnezzar had been on his throne for more than a third of a century when, on January 5, 569 BCE, an eclipse darkened the noonday sun over Babylon city. By that date most of his subjects had known no other ruler. Using labor and wealth gained through conquest, Nebuchadnezzar had erected an imposing capital at the waist of the Tigris-Euphrates valley—a city so grandly fortified that two chariots could pass on the road that ran atop its defending walls. He was, in his time, the dominant ruler in the Middle East. Three times—in 597, 587, and about 573—the Babylonians had conquered Judah and Jerusalem. The first two of these occasions are well documented and widely accepted. But the third is different. The previous chapter (titled "The Cyrus Revolt") outlines what we have found about the 573 Egypt-based uprising, its bloody repression in Judah, and the pogrom that followed against the Judean exiles who resided in Babylon. Indeed, after the Israelites retook Judah, Nebuchadnezzar's full wrath at the rebellion in Judah must have been redirected against the Jewish exiles in Babylon. Remembering that Ezekiel was the leading citizen of the community of the Babylonian exiles, let us turn now to substitute kings.

In the ancient Near East, a solar or lunar eclipse was an omen that the ruler had offended the gods. What often followed was a sentence of death upon that ruler, though planet location and favorable shadowing could overcome this omen. However, equally as often portents were unfavorable, so to honor the portents while avoiding the fate, the true king crowned another. That substitute then personally assumed the doom that the gods had decreed upon the ruling king. The replacement's reign was *never ever* longer than one hundred days, and sometimes within that period the authorities dispatched him. (The Babylonians seem to have beheaded their substitutes.) Once the omens had been satisfied, the king could safely return to his throne.

In the unthinkable event that any substitute lived upon the throne past his hundred-day limit, then the eclipse's omens would have returned to the true king, who soon would have been a dead man. Another feature of calculating the substitute's tenure—in Babylon at least—was that the reigning monarch was annually enthroned during the spring New Year's festival. This meant that the substitute must not be allowed to live even an hour into the festival period, lest he become the one who would be enthroned anew. Both Ezekiel and Jehoiachin were to fall under this stricture.

Seventh-century-BCE archives from Nineveh reveal that the Assyrians employed substitute kings.[1] According to Professor Simo Parpola, who edited those archives, the custom was an ancient one, had originated in Babylon, and probably also was practiced by the Neo-Babylonians.[2] In fact, the Assyrians controlled Babylon in the seventh century BCE, and were seating substitute kings on Babylon's throne a scant fifty years prior to the Neo-Babylonian dynasty's founding. Moreover, Babylon's priestly bureaucracy remained in place after that nation had ousted the Assyrians, and bureaucracies do not voluntarily disband. Finally, there is historical evidence that Persian kings, who succeeded the neo-Babylonians, themselves employed substitutes. Understanding why Jesus assumed the Son-of-Man persona depends upon whether the Babylonians used substitute kings. The evidence is that they did.

The Exile period saw eighty-one eclipses over Babylon, but because of rules pertaining to planet location and coverage of the eclipse's shadow, probably just half these eclipses brought substitutes to Babylon's throne. As a matter of interest, 70 percent of those forty-odd eclipses darkened a portion of the moon and 30 percent shadowed the sun, which gives lunar eclipses a better than two-to-one numerical advantage. Because data from the Nineveh archives are so good, we can determine with reasonable accuracy which eclipses during the Babylonian period would actually have seated a substitute on Nebuchadnezzar's throne.[3]

1. Parpola I and Parpola II. The *Excursus* in Part II discusses *sarpuhi*. It and letters to Assyrian monarchs pertaining to substitute kings constitute chapters 7 and 8 of this book.

2. April 29, 2004 email and July 16, 2006 conversation between Preston Kavanagh and Professor Simo Parpola.

3. Bear in mind, however, that Assyrian authorities erred once by seating a substitute king when they should not have done so. The official practice seems to have been

Appendix 2 shows the forty-one eclipses over Babylon that were most likely to have produced a substitute during the sixty years of the Exile. The table also gives our estimate of the probability that a substitute was seated. The date of one of these eclipses (2/19/561 BCE) precisely fits the release from prison of Judah's King Jehoiachin (2 Kgs 25:27–30), which bolsters the argument made elsewhere that Jehoiachin died as a royal substitute for one of Nebuchadnezzar's successors.[4]

Eclipse for Suffering Servant

Sticking with Isaiah's Suffering Servant, an eclipse started things, but which eclipse? The best choice by far is the solar eclipse of January 5, 569, though other possibilities are the lunar eclipses of September 572 and July 569. In time of day, the New Testament almost exactly matches the Old Testament's 569 BCE solar event with its darkness "over the whole land" from the sixth until the ninth hour (Mark 15:33), while Jesus hung on the cross. Its exilic counterpart, the January 5, 569 BCE solar eclipse, started at 12:23 p.m. The eclipse occurred three years after Babylon, working with Judah's neighbors, had crushed the ill-considered uprising in Judah and had retaken Jerusalem. This victory had provided prize prisoners, such as the former King Jehoiachin; the war leader Asaiah; and probably the brilliant Daniel, who had come to manhood in Nebuchadnezzar's court.

By using Word Links, the authors of Isa 52:13–15 announced across the Diaspora that the recent eclipse had triggered substitute kingship and that Babylonian authorities had named their candidate for substitution.[5] Thus, Isa 52:13–15 is a bulletin, and eclipse tables allow us to date it with accuracy. Very likely that Scripture was written within a week or two of the eclipse in January 569. Those three verses are, of course, related to the full chapter which follows, but Isaiah 53 should be considered apart from the Isaiah 52 verses that precede it. And do these three verses announce the identity of the Suffering Servant?

The Isaiah 52 passage, despite having only thirty-six Hebrew text words, produces at least 1,249 Word Links, which is an extraordinary total. About two hundred of these include "son of man" or "sons of men," which were linked with the words בני אדם in Isa 52:14. Remember that each of

---

"better safe than sorry."

4. Kavanagh, *Exilic Code*, 42–61.

5. Kavanagh, *Exilic Code*, 120–21.

those two hundred links constitutes a unique block of words. Duplicate sets were not permitted and would have been disqualified. The probability that this flood of links could be coincidental is infinitesimal. In the book of Ezekiel, the Son-of-Man title appears over and over again. We count ninety-three times. And Word Links aside, any Jew receiving the Isa 52:13–15 bulletin would have identified Ezekiel as the victim as soon as they saw or heard the words "his form [was] beyond that of the sons of men" (v 15). Exiles and Judean residents alike would have known that their prophet Ezekiel was the subject of the biblical text. Today, some people (such as the writer himself, a group like collective Israel, or perhaps a righteous minority thereof) identify the Suffering Servant as an individual.[6] But Word Links show that Ezekiel, the servant, was to die. (This is new information and vital to solving the New Testament's Son-of-Man problem.)

Moreover, the words of Isa 52:13–15 fit well with what we know of substitute kingship and of the Babylonian court. Ezekiel would prosper, because he would have replaced a king of vast wealth. Upon crowning, Ezekiel would also be exalted and lifted up because he was to mount a specially made throne, which, of course, was higher than any other in the palace, and certainly higher than those of the court's puppet kings. Consider Judah's King Jehoiachin, who was later to be a substitute. When he left prison, he received "a seat [throne] above the seats of the kings who were with him in Babylon" (2 Kgs 25:28).

The Isaiah 52 text reads, "So shall he startle many nations; kings shall shut their mouths because of him" (v 15). The many nations that Ezekiel would startle were entities in Babylon's polyglot empire. The kings who would shut their mouths at him were the puppet kings who then (as Judah's King Jehoiachin once had) dwelt in Nebuchadnezzar's palace. They were Babylon's trophies and hostages. Any substitute for Nebuchadnezzar became a king of kings. Verse 14 speaks of the prophet's marred appearance. There could have been some physical malady that contributed to Ezekiel's social isolation during his long exile. Ezekiel's last dated writing was 573, and the fatal eclipse occurred in 569. He probably had to endure the hardships of prison for those four years. In addition, the prophet very likely had been tortured to find whether he was complicit in the invasion of Judah.

From the Babylonians' own standpoint, they could not have made a worse selection for substitute kingship. What they wanted was a compliant political opponent who, after coronation, would swear to assume the

6. Paul, "Isaiah 40–66."

fatal omens that the eclipse had hung upon mighty Nebuchadnezzar, the reigning king of Babylon. Instead, what they got was the most self-reliant, stubborn, eccentric, God-centered prophet that Israel was ever to produce. He had known privation and death. "He was despised and rejected by men; a man of sorrows, and acquainted with grief . . . " (Isa 53:3), and certainly was not esteemed by his countrymen.

But perhaps the authorities were misled. After all, Ezekiel had lived as an exile in Babylonia for many years, and during much of that time had opposed King Zedekiah's plans to align Judah with Egypt and to revolt against Babylon. Also, the prophet very likely opposed rather than supported his countrymen's disastrous foray against Jerusalem in 573. Yet as a reward for his loyalty to Babylon, Ezekiel found himself nominated for execution. His captors, as a matter of routine, staked everything upon his swearing to the eclipse's omens, but Ezekiel previously had lived in utter silence for long periods. In Ezek 3:26, God said to him, "I will make your tongue cleave to the roof of your mouth, so that you shall be dumb . . . " This stricture started when God informed the prophet that Jerusalem was under siege, and he was not allowed to break his silence until he heard of the city's fall (Ezek 24:26). Also, when Ezekiel's torturers interrogated him, they certainly would have bound him, yet he already had prophetically experienced such binding at God's instruction ("O son of man, behold, cords will be placed upon you, and you shall be bound with them . . . " [Ezek 3:25]). Finally, every substitute's swearing ceremony was performed before the idols of Marduk and/or Shamash within the lavish temples of those pagan gods. This would have been utterly anathema to Ezekiel, since no writer in Hebrew Scripture had ever portrayed a loftier vision of the Lord's sacred presence than did the prophet.

Isaiah chapter 52 closes with a perplexing statement: "Kings [presumably the puppet kings in Babylon's court] shall shut their mouths because of him; for that which has not been told them they shall see, and that which they have not heard they shall understand" (Isa 52:15). But there is a plausible explanation. The Isaiah writer hints in his text that Ezekiel had already determined not to assume the eclipse's omens which overshadowed Nebuchadnezzar. Those puppet kings thought that Ezekiel would comply with the givens of substitution, as had all previous temporary kings. They imagined the prophet would submit, live out his short time, and die in a way that brought honor to his subject people. Then the captive kings could return to the business of haggling over minor marks of status, or whatever else filled their days. However, the writer of Isaiah 52's closing lines must have known that Ezekiel would refuse to lift Nebuchadnezzar's death sentence unless the monarch released every Israelite prisoner taken in the Jerusalem rebellion and during the Babylonia pogrom. Such a holdout by a substitute was beyond imagining.

Simo Parpola's work shows that the ritual carried within itself a sequential flaw. The substitute was first enthroned, and then immediately afterward was forced to swear before the god Shamash (or Marduk) to the written omens and portents that overhung the true king. But enthronement preceded swearing, and if the new king refused to swear, the true king faced death with the fatal omens still attached to him. The substitute Ezekiel could cause Nebuchadnezzar to confront death.

Isaiah 53 Describes Substitute Ritual

We turn now to Isaiah 53—perhaps the most important chapter in Hebrew Scripture, though at the same time one of the most baffling. No scholar has yet identified the so-called Suffering Servant nor explained the historical circumstances under which the servant died.[7] Isaiah 52:13–15, the short passage that preceded Isaiah 53, was a bulletin which announced that, in the stead of Nebuchadnezzar, Ezekiel was to die as a substitute king. However, the text of Isaiah 53 is different. It was written somewhat after Ezekiel's execution, and reflects upon the significance of the Suffering Servant's death.

Encoding supports the choice of Ezekiel as the Lord's Servant. An unusual example is that Isa 52:13's second word and Isa 53:12's last word start or finish significantly coded spellings of "Ezekiel the substitute king" and "Ezekiel," respectively. Thus, Scripture's Suffering Servant passage, Isa 52:13—53:12, starts and ends with Ezekiel's encoded name. The opening encoding stretches over fifteen text words, and is particularly strong.

---

7. Professor John H. Walton of Wheaton College is a partial exception. He has written: "the imagery, background, and obscurities of the Fourth Servant Song can be adequately resolved when the passage is read in the light of the substitute king ritual." "Substitute King Ritual in Isaiah 53," 734. Also, a century ago, R. Kraetzschmar footnoted the "extraordinary similarity" between Ezekiel and the Suffering Servant. Kraetzschmar "thought it strange that no one had so far conjectured that Ezekiel was the 'historical original' of the Servant." Kraetzschmar, *Ezechiel*, 46, n 3, cited by C. North, 56. According to North's note on page 98, by 1900 Kraetzschmar had completed a monograph on Isaiah 53 that connected Ezekiel and the Suffering Servant. However, Kraetzschmar died soon afterward, and the monograph never appeared.

Other encodings—"Son of Man," "Ezekiel the substitute king," and "Ezekiel šar pūḫi,"—were scattered throughout chapter 53. These are noticeable, but not outstanding in probability. The best proof so far that Ezekiel is the Suffering Servant lies in the remarkable Word Link results from the Isaiah 52 verses rather than from the encoding in Isaiah 53. To give footing to this finding, we turn to origin, date, and authorship.

Encoding in Isaiah 53, though not decisive, does provide clues as to the place of origin. Among place names, Migdol Eder has the best coded showing. In fact, Jeremiah addressed two of his pronouncements to exiles at Migdol (Jer 44:1, 46:14). The authors of Isaiah 53 could well have journeyed from Babylonia to Migdol once they had gained release from prison. Probably this was in northern Egypt. Alternatively, there was a Migdol Eder (the "tower of the flock") east of Bethlehem. It became known as a place where the messiah would manifest himself.[8] However, the more probable destination for the released Judeans is in Lower Egypt at a fortress near the Mediterranean. It was one of the centers of residence for exilic Jews. For dating Isaiah 53, let us assume the locale of composition is Migdol in Egypt, and then allot time for travel from Babylon, as well as for recovery, reflection, and writing—three years at the outside, more probably two. Starting with the solar eclipse early in 569, and with several years added to that, a reasonable range for dating Isaiah 53 is between 568 and 566 BCE. By contrast, the Isa 52:13–15 bulletin was composed just after the 569 eclipse, so the gap between the texts could be one to three years. This is some thirty years earlier than "the vast majority of scholars today," who choose the 540s as the time of composition.[9]

Daniel's Authorship

As to possible authorship of chapter 53, coding gives us two strong possibilities, of almost equal weight. The first is Daniel, even though many think him to be a mythical character. But he was very much a real person, one who was active during the Exile. Encoding shows that Daniel (and Belteshazzar, his Babylonian name) was at the very least an author or—much less likely—was a major subject of the Second Isaiah chapters.

He contributed mightily to Scripture, and certainly was an exilic leader. Probably the Babylonians took him prisoner when they recaptured

8. Liid, "Tower of Eder," 284.
9. Clifford, "Second Isaiah," 493.

Jerusalem in 573. It follows that Daniel was one of the exiles freed by Ezekiel as an aftermath of the prophet's substitute kingship, which tilts Daniel's role in Isaiah 53 towards authorship. The account of the Suffering Servant is so compelling that it very likely was written by someone who was liberated from Babylonian imprisonment by the Suffering Servant's sacrifice. Also, whoever wrote the chapter plainly had known Ezekiel during the decades that Ezekiel lived in Babylonia. Given his brilliance and writing skills, Daniel certainly fits.

And could Daniel himself have been the Suffering Servant? We think not. Isaiah 53 well describes Ezekiel, and Daniel not at all. The Servant was despised and rejected by his fellows, and had no form, comeliness, or beauty that his countrymen could admire. That sounds like Ezekiel. On the other hand, Daniel was a youthful prodigy, handsome, nobly born, and endowed with knowledge and understanding (Dan 1:3–4). Also, in adulthood he became a major contributor to Hebrew Scripture, helping to write the Deuteronomistic History. Whomever Isaiah 53 described, it certainly was not Daniel.

Daniel was not the Suffering Servant, though he was a substitute king. We have nearly irrefutable evidence of this! Encodings of "Daniel *šar pūḫi*," "Daniel the *šar pūḫi*," and "Daniel substitute king" undergird the lovely words of Psalm 23. Forty-five encoded spellings of nine different athbash versions of the three are wedged into just fifty-seven Hebrew text words. The probability that these forty-five spellings are coincidental is zero.[10] Daniel the substitute king is clearly the concealed subject of Psalm 23. The psalm certainly lends itself to interpretation as a substitute king text. The subject ate in the presence of enemies (his retinue of armed guards), his cup (of poison) overflowed, and he walked through the valley of the shadow of death (perhaps when his coronation parade passed through Babylon's massive Ishtar Gate).

Returning to Isaiah 53, if Daniel wrote it, he did so before he himself was again in Babylonian hands, and thus subject to enthronement and execution. As we reason it, this is how Daniel might have come once again to be a Babylonian prisoner. When the Suffering Servant forced Nebuchadnezzar to release his Judean prisoners, he also must have secured the safety of King Jehoiachin, and quite probably of Daniel as well, both

---

10. Using chi-square, the probability of these 45 coded spellings appearing within the 57 text words of Psalm 23 is zero. The remaining 5,577 encoded spellings are distributed among the rest of Scripture's 305,439 text words.

of whom had been leaders of the Jerusalem revolt. A few years later, after the death of King Nebuchadnezzar in 562, Daniel probably thought that he could safely return to Babylon. However, Nebuchadnezzar's son Evil-Marduk, who had succeeded his father, reneged on the promise to protect King Jehoiachin, and in 561 executed him as a substitute king.[11] In August of the same year, another killing eclipse occurred, and quite possibly this time it was Daniel who took Evil-Marduk's place upon Babylon's throne.[12] When we learn how to date Psalm 23, we probably can test this. Until we do, this seems a plausible scenario for how Daniel might have written Isaiah 53 and later died as a substitute king.

Besides Daniel, the other nominee for authorship of Isaiah 53 is Jehizkiah, son of Shallum. The coding strength of Jehizkiah's name within the chapter's text is equal to the coding for Daniel-Belteshazzar. (Daniel's Babylonian name was Belteshazzar.) Daniel and Jehizkiah stand alone. Scripture openly mentions the name Jehizkiah just once, in 2 Chr 28:12. He was one of those who intervened with King Pekah of Samaria to release Judean prisoners taken in battle. This cannot be accidental. Never mind that the intervention ostensibly took place centuries before the events of Isaiah 53, or that the Chronicles passage was written a century or so later. The following text from Chronicles describes Jehizkiah's work. "And the men . . . took the captives, and . . . they clothed [Daniel anagram] all that were naked among them; they clothed [Daniel anagram] them, gave them sandals, provided them with food and drink, and anointed them; and carrying all the feeble among them on asses, they brought them to their kinfolk . . . " (2 Chr 28:15). The strong Jehizkiah encoding within Isaiah 53 and the singular appearance of Jehizkiah's name in the Chronicles passage cannot be coincidental. We could well be reading an account of what the Suffering Servant's redemptive death made possible. Also notice the two Daniel anagrams within the Second Chronicles verse. Surely there is room in this most important chapter, Isaiah 53, for both Jehizkiah and Daniel.

But more on Jehizkiah. The name Ezekiel means "God strengthens," and Jehizkiah can be interpreted as "Yahweh strengthens me."[13] Perhaps the Chronicles author is hinting broadly to insiders that the prophet Ezekiel himself, rather than someone born far earlier named Jehizkiah, was the

---

11. Kavanagh, *Exilic Code*, 53.

12. As appendix 3 shows, the next eclipse to bring a substitute to the throne occurred five years later, in 556.

13. Lowery, "Jehizkiah," 658.

one responsible for caring for the enfeebled prisoners. If this is the case, the coauthor Jehizkiah merges into Isaiah 53's true subject, Ezekiel the prophet. The secret of the Suffering Servant's true identity may have been so closely held that even the encoding of the servant's true name had to be altered. If so, then Daniel alone emerges as the leading author of this most important chapter in Hebrew Scripture. Pretty clearly, Jehizkiah son of Shallum was charged with removing the captives from prison and ministering to their needs. This could explain why we have come across no other Hebrew Scripture texts with Jehizkiah encodings. Maybe Jehizkiah was a doer rather than, alas, a writer.

If Daniel, and perhaps Jehizkiah, were the concealed authors of Isaiah 53, did that work name any transgressors? Who decided to mount the ill-conceived campaign to retake Jerusalem? The slender Isaiah chapter contains no fewer than six anagrams of Jehoiachin, the exiled king of Judah. Here they are in the RSV text: "For he grew up before him like a young plant [Jehoiachin anagram]," "Surely he has borne our griefs and carried our sorrows [Jehoiachin]," "But he was wounded for our transgressions [Jehoiachin]," "stricken for the transgression [Jehoiachin]," "was numbered with the transgressors [Jehoiachin]," and "made intercession for the transgressors [Jehoiachin]" (Isa 53:2, 4, 5, 8, 12, 12). Jehoiachin did indeed grow up in Babylon "like a young plant," for he was only eighteen when taken into captivity. He subsequently reached adulthood in Nebuchadnezzar's court and, years later, after his capture at Jerusalem, probably had his eyes put out. Such was the Babylonian custom for oath-breakers.[14] The final verses of Second Kings give an account of Jehoiachin's honorable discharge from prison in 560 BCE, but this misleads. He actually was released to die as a substitute king, and he did.[15]

It is revealing that so many Jehoiachin anagrams are spelled within the word "transgressor." In the 570s, Jehoiachin accompanied the Cyrus-led expedition to recapture Jerusalem, probably with the expectation of resuming his long-interrupted reign as king of Judah. He would have strongly supported the ill-considered campaign, and in the eyes of his countrymen had more than earned his six "transgressor" anagrams in Isaiah 53.

Professor Simo Parpola is an expert on all things Assyrian—including substitute kings. Portions of his seminal work are yet to come within this

---

14. The Babylonians previously had blinded King Zedekiah for his rebellion against them (2 Kgs 25:7).

15. Kavanagh, *Exilic Code*, 42–61.

book. He has written that the particular eclipse announced "the fate decreed to the ruling king *personally* as a punishment for his conduct as king ... It could only be evaded by having somebody to take upon himself the signs sent to the king, to accept responsibility for the king's sins, to be atoned only by death. Thus, the function of the substitute king was basically that of a *scapegoat*, the innocent sufferer, not that of a puppet king."[16] The term "scapegoat" could well describe the situation of any Babylonian substitute king—King Nebuchadnezzar was guilty and the substitute scapegoat had to assume that guilt. But in this single case, this one exception to all other Babylonian substitutions, the true guilt that brought Ezekiel to his throne shifted from the reigning king to rest squarely upon the Israelites—upon those who had mounted the foolhardy expedition to liberate Jerusalem. The ringleaders certainly included the chapter's author, Daniel, and the erstwhile King Jehoiachin, who has six anagrams within Isaiah 53. But we know from other sources that Cyrus the Persian, Queen Mother Huldah, Jeremiah's scribe Baruch, Asaiah the military leader, and Jacob the likely Second Isaiah also led the Judeans who rebelled, and who captured and then briefly held Jerusalem. These were the guilty ones, the people for whom the first Son of Man was to die.

According to the originating text in Leviticus, the scapegoat carried "all the iniquities of the people of Israel, all their transgressions [Jehoiachin and Asaiah anagrams], and all their sins [Cyrus anagram] ... " (Lev 16:21). Professor Parpola certainly chose the correct term in "scapegoat," but he did it without knowing that exilic editors had doctored (or written) the Leviticus passage about scapegoats. Jehoiachin, Asaiah (a military leader), and Cyrus were secretly named! And whom did the Isaiah 53 master name as the guilty ones? "Surely he has borne our griefs [Jehoiachin anagram] and carried our sorrows; yet we esteemed him stricken [Daniel], smitten by God, and afflicted. But he was wounded for our transgressions [Jehoiachin, Daniel], he was bruised for our iniquities ... " (Isa 53:4–5).[17] The Leviticus scapegoat passage earns yet a final look. Perplexingly, the scapegoat is set free carrying the iniquities of all the people of Israel: "The goat [Asaiah anagram] shall bear all their iniquities upon him to a solitary land; and he shall let the goat [Asaiah] go in the wilderness" (Lev 16:23). However, when we interpret the Leviticus passage with what we now know of Isaiah 53,

---

16. Parpola II, XXIV–XXV (Parpola's italics).

17. The second Daniel anagram was of Koheleth, which probably was a commonly used alternative for Daniel.

letting the scapegoat go becomes an apt parallel. The freed captives, redeemed by the Son of Man's suffering and death, departed from Babylon for the wilderness and eventually arrived at Migdol Eder, either in Judah or in Upper Egypt.

At first, Daniel, Jehoiachin, and the other prisoners thought that Ezekiel was undergoing extraordinary pain because God had willed it. That was indeed true, since Ezekiel was following God's will in holding out against extreme torture. But the prophet's purpose was this: the Son of Man refused to swear to the eclipse's omens until Nebuchadnezzar had freed *all* the Israelite prisoners—the rebels captured at Jerusalem and the exiles taken in the Babylonia pogrom. This was life, not theater. Nebuchadnezzar's very life was at stake, and he well understood that time was running out. As far as we know, no previous substitute had dared demand a condition of any sort, let alone one that so defied his captors. Quite possibly, the torturers who initially failed to extract Ezekiel's sworn agreement were themselves put to death. Any new set would also have been charged with keeping Ezekiel alive, however extreme their measures, so that he could swear to the omens.

The Israelites who watched the process at first misunderstood. Initially, they thought that the suffering of the scraggly, aged prophet was punishment he deserved—suffering divinely meted out. But gradually they came to know differently: "We esteemed him stricken [Daniel anagram], smitten by God, and afflicted. But he was wounded for our transgressions [Daniel and Jehoiachin anagrams] . . . upon him was the chastisement that made us whole, and with his stripes we are healed . . . The LORD has laid on him the iniquity of us all" (Isa 53:4–6). Those freed came to understand that the Son of Man's death was redemptive. After reflection, Daniel wrote that the Servant was "stricken for the transgression of my people" and "he poured out his soul to death, and was numbered with the transgressors; yet he bore the sin of many, and made intercession for the transgressors" (Isa 53:8, 12). According to Shalom Paul, "What makes this servant song sui generis is the idea of suffering for another. The servant bears the sins of many, and because of his afflictions the multitude is forgiven."[18] The travails of the first Son of Man were redemptive, and God determined that this be so. Verse 10 says, "It was the will of the LORD to bruise him; he has put him to grief." At last this puzzling chapter has a solution. Ezekiel was the Suffering Servant. Enduring torture, the first Son of Man's holdout against

---

18. Paul, "Isaiah 40–66."

substitute kingship enabled him to secure pardon for his rebellious Israelite countrymen. Understanding this opens the rest of Isaiah 53 to us.

"By oppression and judgment he was taken away," says 53:8. The substitute king process was unjust. It certainly was "oppression and judgment" when the Babylonians used substitution to kill the servant. In addition, some exegetes agree that authorities took the servant from prison.[19] That certainly was where the Babylonians held Ezekiel, and also the Nineveh letters show that the Assyrians stockpiled candidates in confinement pending the next eclipse.[20]

Isaiah 53:10 says, "When he makes himself an offering for sin," and "By his knowledge shall the righteous one, my servant, make many to be accounted righteous; and he shall bear their iniquities." This exactly fits the substitute model. He agrees to become a sin offering and by doing so covers the sins of the many Judean prisoners. Here, according to Parpola, are reports to Assyrian monarchs.[21] "The substitute king of the land of Akkad [Babylon] took the signs on himself." The signs, of course, were evil portents. And, "I made him recite the scribal recitations before the Sun-god, he took all the celestial and terrestrial omens on himself . . . " This ritual transferred the eclipse's evils to the substitute. To paraphrase Isaiah 53, the substitute became an offering for sin, made many righteous, and bore their iniquities.

After Nebuchadnezzar agreed to free the captive Judeans from his prisons, Ezekiel consented to swear the substitute king's oaths and briefly fill that office. Then he was done to death, probably by beheading. The final ceremonies followed. Isaiah 53:9 says, "They made his grave with the wicked and with a rich man in his death." At last this enigma, too, has a solution. After conducting a king's funeral, the executioners buried the servant at the same place and with the same honors given other Babylonian royalty. To the exiles from Judah, royal Babylonians were both rich and wicked. A description of the burial of a Babylonian king's mother during the Exile period follows.[22] King Nabonidus "laid her body to rest wrapped in fine wool garments and shining white linen. He deposited her body in a hidden tomb with splendid ornaments of gold set with beautiful stone beads, containers of scented oil . . . " Kings and governors came from across

---

19. Thomas, "Recent Isaiah 53 Study," 84; Driver, "Servant of Lord," 94.

20. The Persians also kept prisoners for future substitute kings, or at least took substitutes from prisons. See Parpola II, XXX–XXXI (items 15, 16).

21. Parpola I, 21, 227.

22. Pritchard, "Mother of Nabonidus," 561–2. Translator's marks omitted.

the empire to grieve, and the Babylonian people had a period of mourning. Ezekiel's funeral may have been similar. But in Isaiah 53, the Hebrew author turned a ritual for pardon of a pagan king into a rite of pardon for a guilty, subject people.

Even more to the point is the tale of an actual substitute king's final rites. It reports on the burial of the son of Accad's (i.e., Babylon's) bishop, who was made a substitute to govern both Assyria and Babylon. Assyria ruled the two kingdoms, and so named one substitute for both if the eclipse's shadow covered the necessary quadrants. The document is *LAS* 280, addressed to Esarhaddon in early 670 BCE.[23]

> "Good health to the king, my lord ... Damqî, the son of the bishop of Akkad, who had ruled Assyria, Babylonia, and all the countries, died with his queen on the night of the .. th day as a substitute for the king, my lord, and for the sake of the prince Šamaš-šumu-ukīn. He went to his destiny for their ransom. We prepared the burial chamber. He and his queen have been decorated, treated, displayed, buried and wailed over. The burnt-offering has been burnt, all omens have been canceled, and numerous apotropaic rituals, *bīt rimki* and *bīt salā mê* ceremonies, exorcistic rites, *eršaḫunga*-chants and scribal recitations have been performed in perfect manner. The king, my lord, should know this."

The holiest day of the year for practicing Jews is Yom Kippur, the Day of Atonement. The Book of Leviticus directs Aaron: "He shall make atonement ... because of the uncleannesses of the people of Israel, and because of their transgressions [Daniel, Jehoiachin anagrams], all their sins [Cyrus anagram]; and so shall he do [Asaiah anagram] for the tent of meeting ... " (Lev 16:16). With encodings like that, Yom Kippur must have its origin in the 573 Jerusalem disaster, which led to Ezekiel's execution as a substitute king. In those few text words, writers named some of the guilty: Daniel, Jehoiachin, Cyrus, and Asaiah. For good measure, the Leviticus 16 authors inserted no fewer than fourteen Asaiah anagrams, thirteen Huldah ones, and eight for Ezra! This repetition richly earns its exclamation point. One hopes that scholars, certainly the Jewish ones among them, will investigate anew the beginnings of this most sacred day.

---

23. Slight changes in punctuation have been made for easier reading.

Suffering Servant's Eternal Life

Returning to the Isaiah 53 text, there was one final thing—something to be debated to this day. Isaiah 53:10 reads, "When he makes himself an offering for sin, he shall see his offspring, he shall prolong his days." These words pledged that the slain prophet was to see his descendants. How could this be if the decapitated Ezekiel was stone dead and royally buried? And what are we to think about seeing his offspring? The book of Ezekiel relates that the prophet's first wife died (Ezek 24:18), but it adds nothing about children. Scripture, however, implies by "he shall see his offspring [seed]" that he had at least a single child, perhaps more than one—and moreover, that he would see them after his own death.

But what Babylonian ruler would have allowed the son or daughter of a substitute king to survive? The belief was that the replacement monarch actually reigned as a king of Babylon. Any substitute's child, therefore, became a prince or princess of the realm. It seems not only reasonable but highly likely that the authorities executed Ezekiel's children along with him. The Babylonians were no more squeamish than the Assyrians about killing innocents. The Assyrian letters reveal that for each substitute king, a substitute queen was appointed and subsequently slain. Surely the Babylonians also did the same, and very likely they also executed the children of the new king. After all, would any neo-Babylonian king allow free reign in the palace for the legitimate child of a previous monarch? If Nebuchadnezzar ordered the death of Ezekiel's children, the phrase about the prophet seeing his offspring seems clear. There was an afterlife, and Ezekiel would see his children in it. Decapitation was not the end; he would survive death.

"He shall prolong his days" on its face also claims immortality for the executed prophet. In common use, the words meant what they said—days would be added to the servant's life. Since this text was written after his death, how could his living be extended—stretched beyond—his mortal end, except by some sort of resurrection? The substitute king context gives even heavier weight to the phrase. This fixed the substitute's length of life to a maximum of one hundred days from the date of the eclipse, though the Assyrian discoveries show that it frequently was less.

In Babylon, the true king was annually crowned anew during the spring New Year's Festival, so any substitute occupying the throne had to be dispatched before the festival began. (Both Ezekiel and Jehoiachin had their hundred-day reigns shortened to suit the start of Nisan.) Alternatively, the convenience of the true king could decrease that number. A letter from an Assyrian official to his king said, "As regards the substitute king about whom the king, my lord, wrote to me: 'How many days should he sit?' ... Now, if the gods are seen in opposition on the 15th day, he could go to his fate on the 16th. Or if it suits the king, my lord, better, he could as well sit the full 100 days" (*LAS* 135). However, *no substitute king was ever allowed to live beyond the hundred-day limit.* After that, kingship would have reverted to the true king. In such a case, the real monarch rather than the substitute would die, because after the hundredth day the substitute relinquished the royal throne.

The author of Isaiah 52 wrote that Ezekiel would "prolong his days." This statement is doubly astounding because of (a) the unbroken substitute king practice of life having an absolute limit on days, and (b) Scripture's claim that, despite his execution, the Son of Man lived on. The Israelite writer, perhaps Daniel, had turned the pagan ceremony into a testament of God's power: "The will of the LORD shall prosper in his hand." And Ezekiel himself, acting within the ancient and murderous ritual for substitute kings, had made the will of the Lord "prosper." The prophet would see his dead children again and, moreover, his days of life would be indefinitely extended—far beyond the hundred-day deadline. The first Son of Man had eternal life! In its comment regarding verse 10, the Jewish Study Bible said that either the servant is "saved from a fate like death, or he is actually ... resurrected. In the latter case, his resurrection is probably a metaphor for the renewal of the nation at the end of the exile."[24] But Ezekiel's life was not saved, and no metaphor seems intended. The first Son of Man had suffered, died, and then lived again. Centuries later, Jesus used the Son of Man's experience to personify his own ministry.

We do not know where Ezekiel got his Son-of-Man caption. But it is plain that Jesus adopted the title because of the nature of the sixth-century prophet's life and death.

---

24. *JSB*, 892.

Chapter 5

Son of Man from Ezekiel Forward

Isaiah chapter 53 had to be clear enough to describe Ezekiel's judicial murder, while sufficiently obscure to avoid provoking the Jews' rulers. Moderns think obscurity triumphed. But at least through New Testament times (a span of *five hundred* years), some always knew that Ezekiel, the Son of Man, had been the Suffering Servant. Our discussion will treat only briefly later texts such as the Parables of Enoch and Wisdom of Solomon. Instead, this chapter will start with the fate of the Son of Man, Ezekiel himself, and proceed from there towards the approaches to the New Testament. The texts cited in this chapter often contain the phrase "Son of Man" (or occasionally "sons of men") combined with references to royalty, celestial bodies, days or years, and death or eternal life. There are a few other Son-of-Man passages with those characteristics in Hebrew Scripture, but these should suffice. Also, readers should remember that "Son of Man" appears almost one hundred times in the book of Ezekiel, though the prophet is seldom featured by those wrestling with the New Testament's Son-of-Man conundrum.

Proverbs 28:16 and Deut 17:20 contain "prolong his days," the same phrase that appears in Isa 53:10. Proverbs said, "A ruler who lacks understanding is a cruel oppressor; but he who hates unjust gain will prolong his days." We take this as friendly to Ezekiel, the newly wealthy king of Babylon. He certainly eschewed riches, however acquired, and did indeed prolong his days. Next, a Deuteronomy verse is a specific charge to a king, which is unusual in Scripture: "And when he sits on the throne of his kingdom" he shall read the words of the book of the law kept by the Levitical priests "so that he may continue long [literally 'prolong his days'] in his kingdom, he and his children, in Israel" (Deut 17:18–20). This same Deuteronomy passage admonishes a king to copy out and then study a law prohibiting multiplication of horses, wives, and treasure. If he walked this narrow line and listened to the Levites, he could prolong his days and those of his children. The children are an important addition, since Isa 53:10 promised the Suffering Servant that not only should he prolong his days but that he would also see his offspring. Both Proverbs 28 and Deuteronomy 17 support the claim that the servant could lengthen his days beyond the invariable substitute king's limit of one hundred, though Deuteronomy had a Levitical string on it.

Another text, Psalm 89, is crowded with sixth-century anagrams, which probably date it. The psalm disputed that the Son of Man yet lived. "Remember, O LORD, what the measure of life is, for what vanity thou hast created all the sons of men! What man can live and never see death? Who can deliver his soul from the power of Sheol?" (Ps 89:47–48). Clearly, the psalmist did not agree with Isaiah 53 that the Son of Man still lived. This next psalm gives the same opinion, though more eloquently: "O LORD, what is man that thou dost regard him, or the son of man that thou dost think of him? Man is like a breath, his days are like a passing shadow" (Ps 144:3–4).

Some passages use Son of Man without reference to numbered days. However, the writers still manage to express their opinions about Ezekiel, the first Son of Man. Take Job: "How can man be righteous before God . . . Behold, even the moon is not bright and the stars are not clean in his sight; how much less man, who is a maggot, and the son of man, who is a worm!" (Job 25:4–6).

Psalm 146 is a peculiar mix. It rejects the idea of eternal life for the servant, while at the same time rejoicing in the release of prisoners. It could have been written quite soon after Isaiah 53, perhaps in 568 BCE. The psalm warns, "Put not your trust in princes, in a son of man in whom there is no help. When his breath departs he returns to his earth; on that very day his plans perish . . . The LORD sets the prisoners free; the LORD opens the eyes of the blind" (Ps 146:3, 4, 7, 8). Jacob and Huldah both are named twice with anagrams, and they may have been the authors. Here is a speculation: Prisoners have been freed; Ezekiel is dead or soon will be; and Daniel is about to write Isaiah 53, which would assign lengthening of days to the executed Ezekiel. Huldah the Queen Mother and Jacob, who is Second Isaiah, were former allies of Daniel. However, they disagreed about whether Ezekiel had been resurrected. This could explain why the psalm speaks of liberated prisoners while denying life after death to the Son of Man.

Another text is Isa 51:12–13. Its author is Jacob-Second Isaiah, who is once again on the negative side of the life-death question: "Who are you that you are afraid of man who dies, of the son of man who is made like grass, and have forgotten the LORD, your Maker, who stretched out the heavens . . . " Was this written after Isaiah 53, which of course introduced the Son of Man's immortality? Possibly so, and perhaps this marks the start of a Daniel-Jacob argument about the significance of Ezekiel's sacrificial death. Second Isaiah could be trying to change the subject from the prophet's immortality to the awesome, eternal Lord of the heavens. The site of the discussion would have been Egypt.

Readers should keep in mind that Daniel, Jacob, and Huldah came to know Ezekiel well. The three spent years together exiled in Babylon with the prophet. However, Ezekiel remained behind when the other three left for Egypt. While they were to lead the attempt to recapture Jerusalem, Ezekiel was to face prison and ultimately execution. Earlier, as Queen Mother (of young Jehoiachin) in Jerusalem, Huldah had led worship of the queen of heaven, who was the supposed consort of Yahweh, and she continued this practice in Egypt. This enraged both Jeremiah and Ezekiel, and Ezekiel, in particular, lashed out at her. A sample of Ezekiel's long chapter 16, written when Huldah was still in Jerusalem follows. "You trusted in your beauty, and played the harlot [Huldah anagram] . . . and lavished your harlotries [Huldah] on any passerby . . . and made for yourself gaily decked shrines, and on them played the harlot [Huldah]; the like has never been nor ever shall be" (Ezek 16:15–16). Into this single chapter Ezekiel poured seventeen such anagrams! His writings circulated throughout the Diaspora, so Huldah had good reason to both fear and hate him. These feelings could have been part of her reason to deny in the psalms she authored that the opinionated Son of Man had attained eternal life. On the other hand, we have statistical evidence that Huldah edited Ezekiel's writings after his death.[1] Still, a man does not stay on good terms with a woman by repeatedly calling her a whore.

Psalm 8 might have been written soon after Ezekiel's enthronement. Though short, the text contains two Cyrus anagrams (which is statistically significant) and two for Daniel. The psalm is simple and magnificent. Its

---

1. Kavanagh, *Huldah*, 45–46.

words convert Nebuchadnezzar's tawdry substitute king drama into a soaring song of praise to "O LORD, our Lord," and a hymn to the Son of Man, who is God's own creation. "When I look at thy heavens, the work of thy fingers, the moon and the stars which thou hast established; what is man that thou art mindful of him, and the son of man that thou dost care for him? Yet thou hast made him a little less than God, and dost crown him with glory and honor. Thou hast given him dominion over the works of thy hands; thou hast put all things under his feet . . . " (Ps 8:3–6). The Son of Man had been made only a little less than the divinity; he ruled over all things. (The prophet, of course, had substituted for the king of Babylon.) Was Ezekiel still alive when Daniel or another wrote these deathless words? Perhaps so, since the prophet probably wore the crown for a few weeks after the authorities relented and agreed to release the prisoners. We credit Daniel with the psalm.

The book of Ecclesiastes (225 BCE) followed the servant's death by some three hundred years. Ecclesiastes used "son of man" often, and frequently the word "sun" was close at hand. For example, "This is an evil in all that is done under the sun that one fate comes to all. Also the hearts of men [sons of men] are full of evil . . . " (Eccl 9:3). That is to say, all die, including Ezekiel, the Son of Man. He was not immortal, and he was evil. Again, "The sons of men are snared at an evil time . . . I have also seen this example of wisdom under the sun" (Eccl 9:12–13). These "sun" and "sons of man" pairings recall the connection between Ezekiel and a solar eclipse.

The following Ecclesiastes quote leaves no doubt as to where its author stands on the question of eternal life for Ezekiel, the Son of Man. "Under the sun . . . the heart of the sons of men is fully set to do evil. Though a sinner does evil a hundred times and prolongs his life . . . neither will he prolong his days" (Eccl 8:9, 11–13). Only now we can understand that "hundred times" is a veiled reference to the substitute's hundred-day reign. "Prolong his days" matches the phrase in Isa 53:10: "He shall see his offspring, and prolong his days." However, the Ecclesiastes text rejects the assertion that Ezekiel, the Suffering Servant, lives on. Lines at the end of Ecclesiastes 8, by the way, sound just like a substitute's final days—banquets and harems, the life of a king, though prior to execution—"for man has no good thing under the sun but to eat, and drink, and enjoy himself . . . " (Eccl 8:15). Perhaps the author had witnessed the drama of an actual substitute king enthronement firsthand, though three centuries after Ezekiel's kingship. It should be added that the writer ignored Ezekiel's sacrifice and held him in low regard.

Sons of men did evil and had evil hearts. They shared with beasts the fate of death (Eccl 3:19). Madness was in the hearts of the sons of men "while they live, and after that they go to the dead" (Eccl 9:3).

Daniel 7's Son of Man

Daniel chapter 7, written around 170 BCE, is "a text almost unequaled for its influence on both Jewish and Christian messianic speculations in the crucial period up to 100 C.E."[2] Daniel had this vision: "Behold, with the clouds of heaven there came one like a son of man, and he came to the Ancient of Days and was presented before him. And to him was given dominion and glory and kingdom, that all peoples, nations, and languages should serve him; his dominion is an everlasting dominion, which shall not pass away, and his kingdom one that shall not be destroyed" (Dan 7:13–14). Several centuries later, Jesus himself would draw upon Daniel 7—and upon Isaiah 53—to express his own selfhood and mission.

The second-century author of Daniel 7 knew at least as much as we do of the controversy about whether the exilic Son of Man gained eternal life. Perhaps that author hoped to avoid criticism by using the single letter which conveyed the meaning "like" or "as" with the Aramaic word for "son." The writer could then argue that someone other than Ezekiel was meant. We must also remember that the original Daniel was the probable author of Isaiah 53 as well as being a substitute king himself, so inclusion of his name would have added weight to the second-century tale.

The Daniel 7 chapter, however, makes no mention of the Son of Man's suffering and execution. Omitting those painful details, Daniel 7 picks up where Isaiah 53 leaves off. The Daniel writing might simply relate what occurred to Ezekiel after his death and following his resurrection. The risen "one like the son of man," is presented before the Ancient of Days and receives everlasting dominion over all earthly things. Informed readers who knew the secrets of Isaiah 53 understood that Ezekiel had already served as king of Babylon, and now in the book of Daniel they learned that he had become king of everything. Remembering that the exilic Daniel may well have written Isaiah 53, it is natural that someone favoring him should continue to narrate what happened to the Son of Man after one "like" him rose from the dead.

---

2. Nickelsburg, "Son of Man," 137.

So far, so good, but suppose the one "like the son of man" refers to a different and probably more recent substitute king than Ezekiel. We know that Jehoiachin and Daniel were substitutes during the Exile, and that Asaiah probably was, too.[3] Also, certainly the Persians and possibly the Saleucids continued to seat substitute kings.[4] If so, Daniel 7 might even refer to one of those subsequent victims. Given all this, we urge scholars to test the Daniel chapter for encodings and anagrams to see whether its words conceal the identity of someone "like the son of man," who, in the second century, might also have been a savior like Ezekiel.

Although this brief chapter brings several new questions to the ongoing discussion of Daniel 7, it also gives scholars firmer ground to walk upon. (This presumes that the "like" or "as" in Daniel 7 means just that. The Son of Man spoken of is modeled on Ezekiel, the original.) This book brings at least three new discoveries to any Daniel 7 discussion. First, just as Ezekiel was, the one "like the son of man" must in life have been an earthly king. Second, like Ezekiel, he had to have been a substitute. And third, like Ezekiel, the Daniel 7 person attained eternal life. It appears that the Son of Man in the book of Daniel is the same person as the Son of Man revealed in the books of Ezekiel and Isaiah. At least for now.

Son-of-Man mentions in works following Daniel 7 do not seem to notice that another Son of Man has come into play. This of course supports that Ezekiel was the focus of the Daniel text, and is possibly determinative. A number of those writings are mentioned below.

The book of Sirach (early second century BCE) stated directly that the Son of Man could not live, and did so even while artfully inserting a solar eclipse: "Human beings [sons of men] are not immortal. What is brighter than the sun? Yet it can be eclipsed" (Sir 17:30–31). Significantly, Sirach agreed with Ecclesiastes and others that the Son of Man was mortal. This has the ring of one side of an ongoing partisan argument about Ezekiel's immortality, conducted occasionally as late as the second century BCE. (Reaching back, connections like this between Son of Man and solar eclipses validate our original choice that a solar event led to Ezekiel's enthronement.)

Tobit (200 BCE) passed along the Son-of-Man secret. The angel Raphael twice said, "'It is good to guard the secret of a king, but to acknowledge and reveal the works of God, and with fitting honor to acknowledge

3. Kavanagh, *Exilic Code*, 42–61.
4. Parpola II, XXIX–XXXII.

him'" (Tob 12:7, 11). Presumably, the angel implied the *substitute* king. However, this is a marginal reference and lacks the required "son of man." For this reason, we have not included Tobit in a table below. A century later, Wisdom of Solomon connected within a few lines "throne," "servants," "sons of men," and "king" (Wis 9:4–7). With qualification, it enlists on the side of an eternal Son of Man: "Even one who is perfect among human beings [sons of men] will be regarded as nothing without ... wisdom." About the same time, First Esdras wrote, "Wine is unrighteous, the king is unrighteous, women are unrighteous, all human beings [sons of men] are unrighteous... There is no truth in them and in their unrighteousness they will perish" (1 Esd 4:37). Wine could be a reference to the drink given to substitutes at enthronement, and mention of women would fit with a substitute's access to the royal harem. Clearly the author stands against eternal life for any sons of men.

The Dead Sea Scrolls (100 BCE and later) argued that the Son of Man had been mortal and imperfect. The Community Rule said, "What is the son of man in the midst of Thy wonderful deeds ... Kneaded from the dust, his abode is the nourishment of worms."[5] And the Scrolls' Hymn 12 says, "Righteousness, I know, is not of man, nor is perfection the way of the son of man."[6] Since other Essene writings show that the group believed in bodily resurrection and eternal life, this is an especially strong condemnation of the Son of Man.[7] Though we lack Son-of-Man quotations from two other major schools of Jesus's time, note that the Pharisees pictured God and man in close relationship in this life and the next, while the Sadducees rejected any resurrection.[8]

Finally, First Enoch (175 BCE–75 CE) wrote, "From the beginning the Son of Man was hidden, And the Most High preserved him in the presence of his (heavenly) host, and revealed him to the elect."[9] Only now can we venture what this may have meant. Isaiah 53 had concealed Ezekiel, the Son of Man, "from the beginning." Subsequently, God had kept him hidden from all but the elect—those who knew the secrets of the Suffering Servant.

It is time to put these texts in sequential order, and two tables will help to do so. The purpose of this book is to illuminate Jesus's use of the

5. Vermes, *Scrolls in English*, 117.
6. Ibid, 265–66.
7. Collins, "Essenes," 624.
8. Saldarini, "Pharisees," 293; Porton, "Sadducees," 892.
9. Black, *Books of Enoch*, parables 62.6–7.

Son-of-Man title. What Scripture about the Son of Man could he actually have read or heard? Two texts—Isaiah 53 and Daniel 7—are crucial to providing context, and the others discussed above and listed below are important. All involve use of Son of Man coupled with what the authors expressed about the immortality of the Suffering Servant. Dates are estimated but, though interesting, their accuracy is not crucial. Jesus could have been familiar with them all. The two tables below show whether the texts that included Son of Man (or its plural) were hostile to their subject, whether they bespoke royalty, and whether they took a stand on eternal life.

The tables are grouped under the two major sources—Isaiah 53 and Daniel 7—that Jesus may have relied upon for his own Son-of-Man statements. Almost all the passages fall into two time periods—the sixth century and the second–first centuries BCE. Ecclesiastes, a third-century work, is an outlier, but an outlier that treated Ezekiel's sacrifice negatively and with vigor.

Readers might run their eyes over both middle columns labeled "SOM Good/Bad?" These best characterize the pertinent texts. The split is almost fifty-fifty on supporting or denigrating the Son of Man. And those who supported him, in most cases, indicated that he rose to eternal life (six of seven texts). Finally, two-thirds of all the texts admitted that the Son of Man had been regal, as of course Ezekiel was.

Text	Date	SOM Royal?	Mention Heavens or Sun?	SOM Good/ Bad?	SOM Eternal?	Mention Prolong Days?
Isa 52–53	560 BCE	Y	N	G	Y	Y
Prov 28	6th C	Y	N	G	Y	Y
Deut 17	6th C	Y	N	G	Y	Y
Ps 8	6th C	Y	Y	G	Y	N
Ps 89	6th C	Y	N	B	N	N
Ps 144	6th C?	N	N	B	N	N
Ps 146	6th C	Y	N	B	N	N
Job 16	6th–4th C	N	Y	B	N	N
Eccl 3, 8, 9	3rd C	Y	Y	B	N	Y

Earlier Son-of-Man/Substitute King Texts

Text	Date	SOM Royal?	Mention Heavens or Sun?	SOM Good/ Bad?	SOM Eternal?	Mention Prolong Days?
Dan 7	170 BCE	Y	Y	G	Y	Y
Sirach	2nd C	N	Y	B	N	N
1 Enoch	2nd C	N	N	G	Y	N
Wisdom	100 BCE	Y	Y	G	N	N
1 Esdras	100 BCE	Y	N	B	N	N
Scrolls	100 BCE	N	N	B	N	N

Later Son-of-Man/Substitute King Texts

According to Wikipedia, "after 150 years of debate no consensus on the [Son-of-Man] issue has emerged among scholars."[10] However, this book's next chapter will offer what may be an agreeable explanation of why Jesus called himself the Son of Man.

---

10. Wikipedia, Son of man (Christianity).

Chapter 6

Son of Man in the New Testament

THE PURPOSE OF THIS book is to explain how Hebrew Scripture influenced Jesus when he used the Son-of-Man title. Thus far we have established that Ezekiel, the first Son of Man, died as a substitute king and that his death was redemptive. It freed from prison a multitude of Jewish rebels captured by the Babylonians after they had quelled a revolt in Judah. Prior chapters also related that Ezekiel, the Suffering Servant of Isaiah 53, had been granted life beyond death. That sixth-century-BCE prophet used the title Son of Man ninety-three times—more than anyone else in Scripture. The runner-up is Jesus, with eighty-three uses. Scholars, however, have been unable to make a Ezekiel-Jesus connection because (a) no one had worked out that Ezekiel was the Suffering Servant, and thus made Ezekiel's life experience worth considering; (b) Babylonian use of substitute kingship against Judah's sixth-century leaders had not been reckoned with; and (c) the obvious parallels between the apocalyptic Son of Man in Daniel chapter 7 and many New Testament passages led experts to ignore Ezekiel and instead to focus more upon Daniel and nonbiblical sources. Again, this book's purpose is to explain the roots in Hebrew Scripture of Jesus's use of the Son-of-Man title, and the groundwork to do so has now been laid.

However, an impediment to analyzing Son-of-Man passages in the New Testament is that one faces a jungle of parallel, stand-alone, rephrased, and duplicate texts. To lessen the expanse of the thicket, this writer put the eighty-three New Testament Son-of-Man verses in order by composition date. In doing so, we relied upon Marcus Borg's study of the scholarly consensus for dating Mark, Matthew, Luke, John, and other New Testament books.[1] Mark was reckoned at 70 AD, Matthew in the 80s or early 90s, John at about 90, and Luke perhaps at the start of the 90s. Next, we eliminated any duplicate Son-of-Man statements after the first. For example, Mark 2:28 quotes Jesus that the Son of Man is Lord of the Sabbath, and so do Matt 12:8 and Luke 6:5. The wordings of the three synoptic gospels differ only slightly, so we can eliminate the Matthew and Luke verses and retain the one from Mark when considering what sources might have influenced the person who wrote those words.

In another alignment, Mark 8:31 relates "that the Son of Man must undergo great suffering, and be rejected by the elders, the chief priests, and the scribes, and be killed, and after three days rise again." Mark 9:12, 31, and 10:33 have the same meaning and many of the same words, so we can eliminate those three verses, leaving just one to deal with. The same approach works when two of the synoptic gospels share a passage. For instance, Matt 24:27 and Luke 17:24 both speak of the Son of Man coming like a flash of night lightning, so we need only work with the Matthew verse. When finished with comparisons, we had dropped nearly one-third of the New Testament's Son-of-Man verses, leaving fifty-two of the original eighty-three verses to weigh. Appendix 3 shows the eighty-three New Testament verses that contain "Son of Man."

Measuring Influence

And what things should be used to measure influence? Start with Isaiah 53's Suffering Servant, who was Ezekiel. The first Son of Man lived a dedicated life as God's prophet in Babylonia, opposed the revolt in Judah, and was imprisoned. Subsequently, Ezekiel was selected to be a substitute king and, though abused, he refused the crown until the authorities freed his countrymen. His captors then executed him and, after death, his days were extended into eternal life. The New Testament passage quoted above (Mark 8:31) is a nearly perfect fit to its Old Testament cousin. Here is that Mark text again: "The Son of Man must suffer many things, and be rejected by the elders and the chief priests and the scribes, and be killed, and after three days rise again." New Testament passages that include the Son of Man and which mention injustice, suffering, and death clearly bear the Suffering Servant's influence. Indeed, any texts containing the Son-of-Man title that

---

1. Borg, *Evolution of the Word*.

include things done or said by Jesus during his life might qualify and should be considered for Suffering Servant status.

A second choice for influence from the Hebrew Scriptures is Son-of-Man gospel texts that portray a risen king who will forever govern mankind. The predominant influence for such New Testament verses would be Daniel 7. It reads, "Behold, with the clouds of heaven there came one like a son of man, and he came to the Ancient of Days and was presented before him. And to him was given dominion and glory and kingdom, that all peoples, nations, and languages should serve him; his dominion is an everlasting dominion, which shall not pass away, and his kingdom one that shall not be destroyed" (Dan 7:13–14). A New Testament verse like this next one would be an obvious choice for influence from Daniel 7: "The Son of Man will send his angels, and they will collect out of his kingdom all the causes of sin and all evildoers, and they will throw them into the furnace of fire . . . " (Matt 13:41–42).

A third category of New Testament Son-of-Man occurrences includes those that do not fit easily a Suffering Servant or a cloud-riding, apocalyptic Son of Man. We assigned only a half dozen verses to this section out of eighty-three, but could be persuaded to either add or subtract from that figure. For example, what should one do with "the Son of Man is LORD even of the Sabbath" (Mark 2:28)? Is Jesus displaying earthly or heavenly power? In this instance, we added this verse to the total for Isaiah 53 influence.[2]

The following passage from the gospel of John seemed to fit either Son-of-Man model, or perhaps neither of them: "The hour has come for the Son of Man to be glorified" (John 12:23). This verse ended within the total labeled "questionable."

Before considering the texts, we ask the reader to examine this table. It gives an overall view of which sort of Son-of-Man verses are favored by the synoptic gospels and by the remainder of the New Testament books. The choice is between Isaiah 53's tormented but resurrected Son of Man and Daniel 7's unearthly king of kings.

---

2. This was the only Son-of-Man passage in Mark that the Jesus Seminar scholars considered might have originated with Jesus. Funk and Hoover, *Five Gospels*, 49.

Favors	In Mark	In Matt	In Luke	In Other	Total
Isa 53	10	13	12	5	40
Dan 7	4	13	14	6	37
Neither		1	1	4	6
Total	14	27	27	15	83

New Testament Son-of-Man Verses Influenced by Isaiah 53 and Daniel 7

There are eighty-three Son-of-Man verses in the New Testament, with four-fifths of them in the synoptic gospels. The influence in those verses of Isaiah 53's Suffering Servant is slightly greater than that of Daniel 7's kingly figure. Mark is heavily tilted towards an earthly, suffering Jesus. That gospel has ten Isaiah-type references, while only four Son-of-Man verses show the Daniel kind of persona. Assuming that the gospel of Mark most closely described Jesus's view of himself and of his ministry, we conclude that he thought of himself first as one who suffered to deliver others. But note that the Mark author also included four Son-of-Man sayings that favored the risen Christ returning in power with angels.

The Son-of-Man verses in Matthew are evenly split between the two types of savior, thirteen to thirteen, and the Luke emphasis is almost so at twelve Isaiah-type verses to fourteen stressing Daniel. It bears emphasizing that around half of both Matthew's and Luke's Isaiah 53-type texts were not borrowed from Mark, but were either independently derived or shared only between Matthew and Luke. In the table above, verses in the "other" category come mainly from John, the fourth gospel, and these, too, are nearly evenly divided by type of influence, though John has a larger portion of inconclusive verses. The table does not show this, but Matthew and Luke use all but three of Mark's Son-of-Man phrases. The exceptions are all suffering Jesus references (Mark 9:12, 10:45, and 14:41). However, the two later gospel writers also showed considerable independence in adding their own Son-of-Man verses, with ten and eleven apiece, respectively.

Of course, both Matthew and Luke have in common some eight instances that Mark's gospel lacks. Perhaps the best explanation for this is to refer to it as "Q Source material"—an invented term that tags material not found in Mark but which appears in Matthew and Luke. The eight instances are equally divided between verses that could have been influenced either by Isaiah 53's Son of Man or by Daniel 7's. Four Q Source references associated with the Suffering Servant are: the Son of Man is termed a "glutton" and a "drunkard" (Matt 11:19 and Luke 7:34), the Son of Man will suffer at their hands (Matt 17:12 and Luke 17:25), the Son of Man came to save the lost (Matt 18:11 [an omitted verse] and Luke 19:10), and the Son of Man has no place to lay his head (Matt 8:20 and Luke 9:58). Looking backwards, the no-place-to-lay-his-head verse hints that Ezekiel, the first Son of Man, was a fugitive before the Babylonians captured him. Given our present task, this must be no more than an alert to those who may seek answers about Ezekiel using Word Links, encoded writing, and anagrams.

To trace influences, so far we have emphasized the differences between the Isaiah 53 and the Daniel 7 types of Son of Man. Some three and one-half centuries separate those two texts, which is a lot. Are all the passages of both types about Ezekiel? Probably Ezekiel was the model for both. In the Daniel text, a single letter conveys the meaning "like" or "as" with the Aramaic word for "son." The author could have been telling learned readers that one "like the son of man" sat at God's right hand—a substitute king who had been sacrificed more recently than the sixth century. An expert states that "a transcendent judge and deliverer was a known element in Jewish eschatology by the latter part of the 1st century C.E."[3] Looking at Daniel 7, we could easily move that date back to the second century BCE, or even earlier. What we do not know yet is whether the Persians or the Seleucids (both of whom succeeded the Babylonians) continued to execute substitute kings. If they did, the figure whose "dominion is an everlasting dominion" might be a different person than Ezekiel. If, however, the Daniel 7 Son of Man represented the risen Ezekiel, then it was he who sat at the right hand of the Ancient of Days. The synoptic gospels, especially Mark, deftly and certainly fix the Ezekiel model of the Suffering Servant upon Jesus. Or, to speak more particularly, Jesus himself *as remembered by others* applied his inward knowledge about the first Son of Man as he fulfilled his passion as the second Son of Man.

Update Jesus Seminar Ratings?

All of this, however, is not a measure of the authenticity of Jesus's own words and words about him. Much of that work has been done by the Jesus Seminar, a group of scholars who discussed and then voted, passage by

3. Nickelsburg, "Son of Man," 141.

passage, in a book called *The Five Gospels* (so-called because it included Thomas). More than seventy biblical scholars labored for six years on the task. What an achievement! They rated each line, verse, or passage in four stages, from "Jesus undoubtedly said this or something like it" to "Jesus did not say this; it represents the perspective or content of a later or different tradition."[4] A similar range was used for items that were not quotations, starting with "I would include this item unequivocally in the database for determining who Jesus was" and finishing with "I would not include this item in the database."[5]

How did the gospels' Son-of-Man passages fare when closely examined by such august experts? The answer is badly, very badly. Sticking with Mark, the scholars voted that just two of those fourteen verses contained any Jesus content at all, and neither obtained a top grade. To repeat that bad news, the scholars rated only two of Mark's Son-of-Man passages as being connected with Jesus, however distantly. The two were "The Son of Man is LORD even of the Sabbath" and "The Son of Man came not to be served but to serve, and to give his life as a ransom for many" (Mark 2:28, 10:45).

Here is a summary so far. Around 573 BCE, Nebuchadnezzar crushed a Cyrus-led revolt that had captured Jerusalem. The uprising led to a persecution in Babylonia, and Ezekiel and many others were captured and imprisoned. Ezekiel, of course, bore the title Son of Man. After a midday solar eclipse on January 5, 569, Ezekiel was selected to serve and to die as a substitute for the Babylonian king. Despite being tortured, however, the first Son of Man refused to accept the supposed burden of the eclipse's deathly omens until Nebuchadnezzar had released the Jewish prisoners captured at Jerusalem and within Babylonia. Working against a deadline of one hundred days, Nebuchadnezzar finally relented, ordered the captives released, and then executed the Son of Man. Clearly, the prophet's death was redemptive. Ezekiel, the first Son of Man, did indeed give his life as a ransom for many.

Returning to Scripture, the final verses of Isaiah 52 announce—mainly through Word Links—that the prophet had been selected as a substitute for Babylon's king. These text words underlined his selection to contemporaries: "My servant shall prosper, he shall be exalted and lifted up, and shall be very high" (Isa 52:13). On the other hand, Isaiah 53—the entire following chapter—is a description of Ezekiel's travail, death, and

---

4. Funk and Hoover, *Five Gospels*, 36.
5. Ibid.

resurrection: "He was wounded for our transgressions ... he shall see his offspring, he shall prolong his days" (Isa 53:5, 10). Recall that in the context of the substitute ritual, Ezekiel had to die within one hundred days after the eclipse. If he did not, then Nebuchadnezzar's life was forfeit. Barring Nebuchadnezzar's death, there could be no prolongation of days—unless Ezekiel had been raised from the dead. And according to Isaiah 53, he was; his days were prolonged!

Against this background, consider the following three Son-of-Man verses from the second gospel. Mark 8:31 says: "He began to teach them that the Son of Man must undergo great suffering, and be rejected by the elders, and the chief priests, and the scribes, and be killed, and after three days rise again." The Jesus Seminar scholars gave this item a black rating, indicating that it should be excluded when determining who or what Jesus was. They state that even though this forms the basis of Mark's gospel, the words predicted future events. Now, however, we can recognize that this was less a prediction than a reenactment, and of course it seems obvious that Jesus would know that he was putting himself at mortal risk when he entered Jerusalem. The parallel synoptic passage in Luke says this: "The Son of Man must undergo great suffering, and be rejected by the elders, chief priests, and scribes, and be killed, and on the third day be raised" (Luke 9:22). These passages rely, in part, upon Paul's earlier formulation in 1 Cor 15:3–5: "Christ died for our sins in accordance with the Scriptures, and that he was buried, and that he was raised on the third day in accordance with the Scriptures, and that he appeared to Cephus, then to the twelve. Then he appeared to more than five hundred brothers and sisters ... " Paul, the earliest to outline this basic gospel, twice used the term "in accordance with the Scriptures." And Mark 14:49 tells that when armed men seized Jesus on the night of his betrayal, he protested that he was not a bandit. Instead, he instructed his disciples to put up their arms to "let the Scriptures be fulfilled." But what Scriptures might they be?

Two other verses in Mark thumbnail a gospel similar to that which Paul set out. One is "He was teaching his disciples that ... 'The Son of Man is to be betrayed into human hands, and they will kill him, and three days after being killed, he will rise again'" (Mark 9:31). The other text also involves teaching. Jesus says, "See, we are going up to Jerusalem, and the Son of Man will be handed over to the chief priests and the scribes, and they will condemn him to death; then they will hand him over to the Gentiles; they will mock him, and spit upon him, and flog him, and kill him; and after three days he will rise again" (Mark 10:33–34). The Jesus Seminar fellows assign both sayings to Mark himself rather than to Jesus. They say that "Jesus himself did not have specific knowledge of his death" and that "Mark has put his own confession of faith on the lips of Jesus, in accordance with the practice of ancient oral cultures."[6] While these three "gospel" statements may indeed sound overly predictive, Mark, as Paul would have, believed them to be fundamental to describing the persona and mission of Jesus. In view of these new findings, scholars should reevaluate Jesus's declarations concerning the Son of Man. But not yet. Professor Parpola's bedrock findings on Assyrian substitute kings are still ahead.

---

6. Funk and Hoover, *Five Gospels*, 94.

Chapter 7

The Assyrian Substitute King Ritual

WHAT FOLLOWS IS THE most important chapter of this book. It sets forth the writing *Excursus: The Substitute King Ritual,* by Simo Parpola, who held the title of Professor Extraordinary of Assyriology at the University of Helsinki. Portions of his seminal translation of *Letters from Assyrian Scholars to the Kings Esarhaddon and Assurbanipal* (Volume 1), as well as his comments (in Volume 2) about the numerous cuneiform letters that discussed substitute kings, are included in chapter 8 of this book. *Letters* is a two-volume work based on the doctoral dissertation that Professor Parpola completed over forty-five years ago, and the *Excursus* was omitted when the two volumes were subsequently reprinted in 1993.[1] This *Excursus* shows that in the late seventh century BCE, Assyrian kings were enthroning substitutes at Nineveh and in neighboring Babylonia, which they then controlled. These letters, thoughtfully read and matched with Scripture, allow one to conclude that the prophet Ezekiel died as a Babylonian substitute king.

For some years, there has been the danger that biblical scholars would overlook or lose entirely the information Parpola has given us about ancient substitute kings. But by placing this *Excursus* in print once again, we do everything we can to keep alive this precious knowledge about Assyrian and Babylonian substitutes. One hopes that, after considering this *Excursus* and the actual letters to Assyrian kings that follow, readers will reach the conclusion that the Suffering Servant was a substitute king. It follows that Ezekiel, the first Son of Man, died as a Babylonian substitute.

1. The reprinting occurred in 1993 when Helsinki Press published a similarly titled *Letters from Assyrian and Babylonian Scholars*, which omitted the *Excursus* on substitute kings printed in the original volume II, XXII–XXXII. *Letters from Assyrian Scholars* was reprinted in 2007 and is available at www.eisenbrauns.com/item/PAR1LETTER.

Ezekiel to Jesus

Excursus: The Substitute King Ritual

(by Simo Parpola)

By the *substitute king ritual* is understood an arrangement in which, briefly put, the ruling king temporarily abdicates his throne for a surrogate who, having ruled his predetermined period, is put to death, after which the king re-ascends his throne and continues ruling as if nothing had happened. This rite forms the subject of one of the most familiar tales in the Arabian Nights, and from incidental and garbled statements made by ancient historiographers (see below, pp. 70–79) it has long been known (or suspected) that the ritual was from time to time actually practiced in ancient oriental courts. The historicity of these more or less anecdotal reminiscences was put beyond all doubt by the discovery of the Nineveh letter archives, which contain numerous references to a substitute king (*šar pūḫi*) ruling in the king's place, and above all by the publication in 1957 and 1967 of two sets of ritual texts (Akkadian and Hittite) showing that the rite was known and practiced all over the ancient Near East, not just in Sargonid Assyria. These texts revealed many previously unknown facts about the ritual and its function, but they also presented many problems, some of which have proved very difficult to solve. Despite much discussion (see Bibliography under Bottéro 1978, Böhl 1953, Dhorme 1941, Kümmel 1967, Labat 1957/58 and 1959/60, Landsberger 1965, Parpola 1971, Schott 1941–42, von Soden 1936 and 1956), there still exists much unclarity about the exact circumstances calling for the performance of the ritual, about the frequency at which it was performed, and—since the ritual instructions are badly broken—even about the general course of the ritual. This underlines the importance of a thorough and systematic analysis of the information provided by the *LAS* corpus—for the 30 letters of the corpus pertaining to the ritual (*LAS* 25–28, 30–32, 77, 134–139, 166–167, 179,185, 205, 232, 235–6, 249, 257, 278–80, 292, 298–99, 317 and 334) not only are (along with *ABL* 735 and a few administrative documents from Calah, see below, pp. 71–73) the only as yet available *direct* documentation of the performance of the ritual; they also contain a wealth of information furnishing, when properly organized, an answer to all the puzzles it initially presents.

The individual *šar pūḫi* letters are thoroughly analyzed and discussed in the commentary. The present chapter provides, by way of a synthesis, a discussion of the ritual as a whole, and a catalogue of all attested instances of its performance—including ones recorded in non-cuneiform sources.

The numbers in square brackets in the following discussion refer to entries in this catalogue. No systematic stand is taken on the research hitherto done (cf. above), which is taken as the point of departure to the present study.

The ritual: description and discussion

The need for a substitute king was created by evil omens, specifically *eclipses*, portending the death of the king. This is made quite clear by the ritual tablet [3], which defines the cause of the ritual as "the evil portent of evil and unlucky signs, eclipses of the moon, the sun, Jupiter, Venus, Mercury and Saturn, [and Mars]" (A 9–13). In fact, every single performance of the ritual featured in the *LAS* correspondence can be traced back to an eclipse, either a lunar or [11, 13] a solar one. And while no "planetary eclipses" (i.e., occultations of planets behind the moon) can as yet be shown to have triggered the ritual, there is no reason to doubt that they may occasionally have done so (cf. discussion sub *LAS* 14).

Not every eclipse, however, called for the performance of the ritual. One important restriction derived from an omen included in Tablet XX of *Enūma Anu Enlil*: "If an eclipse (of the moon) takes place and the planet Jupiter is present in that eclipse, the king is safe; a noble dignitary will die in his stead." (*ACh* 2 Spl. 29:14)

This omen implied, as pointed out in three messages to the king where it is quoted (*LAS* 298, *ABL* 1006 and *RMA* 272), that there was no need to enthrone a substitute if Jupiter had been visible during the eclipse since the god's presence indicated that the sign did not, as usual, concern the king but one of his magnates. A similar restriction also applied to solar eclipses:

"If an eclipse (of the sun) takes place and Venus and Jupiter are visible, the king is safe, but the country will be attacked by an enemy." (*ACh* Šamaš 8:6, see App. F 4.5)

A further restriction resulted from the analysis of the eclipses themselves. While every eclipse (excepting the cases just mentioned) in principle signified that a powerful king was to die (cf., e.g., *ACh* Spl. 22 ii 4', "If the moon is eclipsed on the 14th of Simānu, a famous king will die", and ibid. iii 12', "If an eclipse occurs from the 1st to the 30th of Du'ūzu, . . . a great king will die"), the identity of the king and the land in question had in each case to be established separately by taking into consideration the month, day, and hour of the eclipse, the area of the moon's or the sun's disc affected by the eclipse, and the direction in which the eclipse shifted (see App. F 4).

Of overriding importance was the message sent by the eclipsed disc, which was divided into four quadrants, each corresponding to a specific quarter of the world (Amurru, Elam, Subartu, Akkad); the other factors were of subordinate interest. The darkening of a quadrant implied a threat to the relevant country. Thus, a total eclipse spelled danger to all kings of the world, while e.g. an eclipse touching only the upper part of the moon or the sun signified that a king of the West (Amurru) was going to die. The kings of Assyria were in danger whenever the lowermost quadrant (Subartu/Assyria) was eclipsed. For Esarhaddon, who was the king of both Assyria and Babylonia, even eclipses with darkened right-hand quadrant (Akkad/Babylonia) posed a mortal danger.

Accordingly, the need for a substitute king theoretically arose in Assyria whenever the portion of the lunar or solar disc representing Subartu (in the case of Esarhaddon: Subartu *and* Akkad) was eclipsed and the planet Jupiter was not simultaneously visible. How this theory was converted into practice can be seen from the following analysis of 16 consecutive eclipses in the reigns of Esarhaddon and Assurbanipal:

Eclipse	Quadrants Eclipsed	Visibility of Jupiter	Substitute King Required (and Attested)
680 Jul 11 / Duz 14	Amurru	–	no
679 Jun 1 / Sim 14	Subartu	–	yes
679 Jun 17 (Sun)	ALL	–	yes (*LAS* 30f.?)
678 May 22 / Sim 14	ALL	+	no (*ABL* 1006, *RMA* 270)
677 Nov 3 / Ara 14	Subartu + Elam	–	yes (*LAS* 136:12)
674 Sep 3 / Ulu 15	ALL	–	yes (*LAS* 30f.?)
673 Feb 27 / Add 14	Elam + Amurru	–	no (*RMA* 272B)
671 Jul 2 / Duz 14	ALL	–	yes (*LAS* 26f., 249, 278, 292)
671 Dec 27 / Kan 15	ALL	–	yes (*LAS* 185, 232, 279f., 317)
670 Dec 17 / Kis 15	Amurru	–	no (*LAS* 41, 62, 164, 173ff.)

Eclipse	Quadrants Eclipsed	Visibility of Jupiter	Substitute King Required (and Attested)
669 May 27 (Sun)	Subartu + Amurru	–	yes (*LAS* 28, 104)
669 June 10 / Sim 14	Subartu	–	yes (*LAS* 25, 77, 234f., 257)
667 Apr 21 / Nis 16	ALL	+	no (*LAS* 40, 61)
667 Oct 15 / Taš 14	ALL	+	no (*RMA* 272A, 273)
666 Apr 10 / Nis 15	Subartu + Akkad	+	no (but enthroned by error! See *LAS* 298)
666 Oct 4 / Taš 14	Amurru + Akkad	–	no

As can be seen, of these 16 eclipses, eight (exactly one half) called for the enthronement of a substitute king in Assyria. In all these cases (insofar as our evidence goes), a substitute was actually enthroned. Conversely, excepting one case explicitly labelled a mistake (*LAS* 298), eclipses interpreted as harmless according to the above principles never triggered the ritual. This veritably perfect fit between theory and praxis proves that the factors considered really played the central role in deciding whether the king needed a substitute or not.

As soon as the need for a substitute had been established, the king was notified. In *LAS* 185 [10] and 134 [9], this was done by the chief exorcist alone, and in *LAS* 28 [11] and 31 [7], by a group of several high-ranking scholars, including the chief exorcist, the chief scribe and the chief chanter. The latter probably was the normal practice (cf. [15]). Note that *LAS* 185 represents a special case, in which the suggestion to enthrone a substitute was exceptionally presented to the king already *before* the eclipse had actually taken place. Normally the need for the substitute could only be determined *post eventum*. In any case, the idea of enthroning a substitute never came from the king himself but from his counselors, even in the abnormal case of [12] (see discussion sub *LAS* 298). And while the king was formally given the option to decide whether the ritual would be performed or not (cf. *LAS* 185 r.17), it was surely taken for granted that the answer was always in the affirmative (cf. [15]!).

Having gotten the go-ahead signal, the chief exorcist picked up a suitable substitute—a prisoner of war [4], a prisoner [15], a criminal condemned to death [16], a political enemy of the king [10], a gardener [1] or a simpleton (*LAS* 280 r.13ff)—in a word, a person whose life did not matter much or who would have deserved death anyway. The man was taken to the palace (*LAS* 279:7, [6]), treated with wine, washed and anointed, clad in the king's robes, furnished with the diadem and other royal insignia, and eventually seated on the royal throne ([1, 15–16, 19]; cf. *LAS* 134 and Ritual Tablet, [3], B 5–6, and see note on *LAS* 185 r.18). A "girl" (*LAS* 139) or "virgin" (Ritual Tablet, Col. A 20) was at the same time seated at his side as his "queen" (cf. [4] and *LAS* 30 and 280), and a statuette was presented as a substitute to the Netherworld gods [4].

At this moment, the substitute and the real king formally reversed their roles. The changed status of the latter is reflected in the fact that after the enthronement of the substitute, he was no more to be addressed as "king" [4] but as "Peasant" or "Farmer" (LÚ.ENGAR, cf. App. L 1 and 6) or simply as "my lord" (*LAS* 26–28). And while relevant evidence is lacking, it seems reasonable to assume that he did not wear any external marks of kingship or go near the throne as long as the substitute was occupying it, and otherwise, too, kept a low profile. It goes without saying, of course, that this reversal of the roles was only symbolic. In the eyes of his aides, the king was still very much the real king, as indicated by several letters (*LAS* 134–136, 249, 278–79 and 292) written while a substitute king was on the throne but nevertheless (inadvertently) addressed to the *king*, not the "farmer".

That the "reversal of roles" was only partial is also indicated by the fact that merely putting a substitute king on the throne was just not enough. One had also to make sure that the fate portended by the eclipse really was to befall him and not the real king, under whose rule the portent had occurred. To this end, the eclipse omens, along with other recently observed evil portents, were written down and (immediately after the enthronement) recited to the substitute king and his queen, who had to repeat them "in front" of Šamaš, the celestial judge (*LAS* 26, 30 and 279). The importance of the recitation ceremony (supervised by the chief scribe and complemented with exorcistic rites) is borne out by the fact that it had to be performed even in the (rare) case when the substitute had been enthroned *before* the eclipse had actually taken place (*LAS* 279). It made the substitute ... "accept" from the officiating scholar the signs that had been originally sent to the king (*LAS* 30). To make sure that the omens would irrevocably remain affecting the substitute, the document where they were written was physically *attached* to his garments (*LAS* 26).

The ceremony just described reveals an important thing about the rationale behind the whole ritual. The danger looming before the king, as portended by the eclipse, was not just something that would befall *any* king [of Assyria]; it was the fate decreed by the gods to the ruling king *personally* as a punishment for his conduct as king. This fate could not be evaded by just suddenly abdicating the throne; it could only be evaded by having somebody ... take upon himself the signs sent to the king, to accept responsibility for the king's sins, to be atoned only by death [4]. Thus the function of the substitute king was basically that of a *scapegoat*, the innocent sufferer, not that of a puppet king. He had to be a king, because otherwise the Scriptures would not come true, but otherwise the aspect of kingship was secondary. The whole ritual was functionally equivalent to the *pūḫi amēli* ("man's substitute") ritual described in commentary to *LAS* 140, in which a virgin kid was sacrificed to save a deadly sick patient. For the aspect of "sin" associated with the ritual cf. discussion sub *LAS* 35 (and 321).

The fate portended by the eclipse was to befall the king within 100 days from the occurrence of the eclipse (see note on *LAS* 135 r.6). Accordingly, the "reign" of the substitute king theoretically could, and in certain cases [9] certainly did last for as long as a hundred days. It could, however, and probably often did end considerably earlier. [10] certainly lasted less than a hundred days, [11] for 47 days, [12] for 20 days, the case planned in *LAS* 205 for only 7 days, and [19] (if the tradition is correct) for only 3 days. This variation in the duration of the ritual shows that the length of the substitute's reign was of no great importance in itself, and depended in each case on external circumstances. For instance, if other eclipses were liable to occur after the eclipse, as in the case of [11], the reign was certain to last for at least a month, so that the "evil" of all potential eclipses would befall the same substitute. If, on the other hand, no eclipses or other unlucky celestial portents were to be expected within a hundred days from the initial eclipse, there was no pressing need to extend the substitute's reign to its theoretical maximum; it was left to the king to decide whether he should "go to his fate" early or "complete his 100 days" (cf. *LAS* 135).

A special case was constituted by eclipses calling for repetition of the enthronement rites. According to *LAS* 298:11f and 9ff., the substitute had to be enthroned in the residence of the ruler. For Esarhaddon (and other Assyrian kings who also held the kingship of Babylon), this meant that each time the lunar quadrant corresponding to Babylonia was eclipsed, a substitute had to be placed on the throne in Babylon as well. And if the quadrants of *both* Assyria and Babylonia were eclipsed, as actually happened three times in Esarhaddon's reign, the *same* substitute had to be enthroned *both* in Nineveh *and* in Babylon. Since the latter city was in ruins and thus not yet suited for a royal residence city in Esarhaddon's reign, the scene of the enthronement rites in Babylonia was in this reign the ancient capital of the Sargonic empire, Akkad (cf. *LAS* 134, 249, 279, 280, 298 and *CT* 53 206; it is uncertain whether Akkad was already the scene of the ritual in *LAS* 30). It seems that in the case of such double enthronements, the reign of the substitute was preferred to extend to its full length. *LAS* 26 indicates that the re-enthronement of the substitute in Akkad took place 50 days after the first enthronement in Nineveh, and *LAS* 292 shows that it ended after the full 100 days, so that the substitute came to spend exactly the same number of days both in Assyria and Babylonia. This appears to have been the case in *LAS* 30, too. On the other hand, in *LAS* 279 [10] the substitute was transferred to Akkad immediately after his enthronement in Nineveh. This may well have been due to the inflamed political situation in Assyria at the moment (cf. commentary on *LAS* 247, and also *LAS* 185 r.25 and 280 r.7ff.).

Until quite recently, nothing certain was known about the status of the substitute king during his "reign". The allegations of the Greek and Persian historians [16, 19] and the tradition of the Arabian Nights that he enjoyed full royal powers is now to some extent confirmed by the Nimrud wine lists published by Kinnier Wilson (5a, 6a). These show that the substitute king had a sizeable entourage, about 1/10 the size of the royal court, which included musicians, cooks, confectioners and other personnel designed to entertain the body and soul of the mock king. The lists also show that a sumptuous banquet (*naptunu*) was a regular feature of the substitute king's day, and that he was (at least in . . . certain measure) able to travel around. But they also reveal something that could not be a priority expected, viz. that as much as 1/3 of the substitute's "entourage" (about 100 men) consisted of bodyguards. Since the real king was certainly not in the least concerned about keeping his surrogate alive, this large number of armed attendants can only have served the function of keeping the surrogate under close surveillance, to prevent any attempt to perpetuate the example set by Illilbāni [1]. It is hence clear that whatever "royal power" the substitute king possessed was only illusory; he seems to have been permitted to display a considerable amount of royal pomp in ... public, and to enjoy a comfortable life, but the real power stayed with the king.

The king himself was certainly, to some extent, inconvenienced by the substitute's reign. Not only was he forced to maintain a costly mock court for the substitute king and to withdraw from public life, but he was also strongly advised to stay within the confines of the palace and not to leave for the open country until the 100-day term of the eclipse was over (*LAS* 280 r.13, 299 r.7). The same injunction also concerned the other members of the royal family (cf. *LAS* 249). Otherwise, however, at least the private life of the monarch seems to have continued as usual. He kept receiving letters and even conducting administrative business with his officials (cf., e.g., *LAS* 278 and 292).

When the time came to terminate the ritual, both the substitute king and his queen were put to death. The ritual tablet [3] prescribes this explicitly ("The man given as substitute for the king will die, and the king and his country will be well", Col. A 6'f.), and all sources attesting to the performance of the ritual (with the understandable exception of [1]) imply the same. Exactly how the substitute met his death is unclear in most instances, and may have varied depending on the case. It is suggested in the commentary to *LAS* 280 that the method preferred in Sargonid Assyria was an overdose of "soporific"; but [16] suggests that harsher methods were normally resorted to, and this may well have been the case. The expression "to go to one's fate" used when referring to the substitute king's death (*LAS* 135, 166, 249, 280 and 292) does not imply that the event itself was a matter which one preferred not to talk about directly, but rather that it was regarded as something decreed by fate and thus not to be avoided. The manner of death did not matter greatly.

The only extant description of the burial of a substitute king is provided by Mār-Ištar in *LAS* 280. This letter tells that the substitute was buried with royal honors. He and his queen were balsamized, bewailed and publicly displayed just like any royal dead (cf. commentary on *LAS* 4 and 195), and their corpses were deposited in a mausoleum (KI.MAH) specifically built for the occasion. A tomb (lit. a "resting place", *maṣallu*) of the substitute king is also mentioned in *LAS* 32. It may be, of course, that the publicity given to the burial of the substitute in *LAS* 280 was exceptional and dictated by the political necessities of the day (cf. ibid., r.8); but the possibility that the burial of the substitute king was a public event comparable to that of the king cannot be excluded for the present (however unlikely it may appear).

At the time of and following the burial many magical rites were performed. The ritual tablet (Col. A 18f.) prescribes the preparation of a figurine of "everything that is evil" *ṣalam mimma lemnu*) which the substitute was supposed to take with himself to the Netherworld. *LAS* 280 states that "all kinds of exorcistic rites, including the elaborate rituals of *bīt rimki* and *bīt salā mê*" (actually prophylactic rites performed on the occasion of an eclipse) were performed at the burial. This may be exaggeration, but both the ritual tablet (Col. B 9ff.) and *LAS* 179 make it clear that the royal exorcists had a lot to do after the substitute's death. The palace of the king had to be surrounded with all kinds of prophylactic figures designed to drive off evil forces threatening the king's peace of mind, and the king himself was to be cleansed immediately after the substitute king had "gone to his fate" (ritual tablet, col. B 8'; *LAS* 166:11; cf. also [15b]). We do not know how this purification was effected (it may have involved a shaving ritual, a bath in the Tigris, the donning of new garments, and a lot of incense burning, or a combination of all these cleansing methods), but it may be assumed that it was at least as much intended to clean the king's conscience as his (probably very little stained) body. One may speculate that the performance of the ritual, which indeed, as often emphasized (cf., e.g., von Soden, 1954, p. 125), came close to a human sacrifice, was bound to leave an undeletable impression on the king's psyche—cf. the testimony of the Alexander biographers, below [15].

Catalogue of sources and references to the ritual

1. Chronicle of the Early Kings (Grayson, *TCS* 5 p. 155, No. 20), A31–36: King Erra-imitti (of Isin, 1868–61) had the gardener Illil-bāni seated on his throne as a substitute statue (NU NÍG.SAG.GIL-e) and he placed his royal tiara upon his head. Erra-immiti died in his palace while swallowing hot porridge. Illil-bāni who was sitting on the throne did not leave it, and was accepted as the king (1860–1837 BC). For royal inscriptions of Illil-bāni see E. Sollberger and J.R. Kupper, *IRSA* p. 179f.

    a. Agathias Scholasticus (died A.D. 582), *Hist.* II 25: As the dynasty of the family of Semiramis ended with this Beleus, a certain man named Belētaras, who was a gardener and the keeper and overseer of the royal orchards, by accident plucked for himself the kingship and founded his own dynasty, as noted by Bion and Alexander Polyhistor (1st cent. B.C.). It is generally agreed (cf. Labat, *RA* 40 124) that this anecdote is based on the chronicle entry just quoted, probably through the intermediary of Berossus. How the name Illil-bāni came to be replaced by Belētaras (= Belē-ēṭer) remains a mystery.

2. The OB/MB epistolary formula *ana dinān bēlīja lullik* "I am ready to die as my lord's substitute" (*CAD* D p. 148 and E. Salonen, *StOr* 37 103f.). Possibly an indirect indication that the ritual was repeatedly practiced in the OB/MB period, cf. *LAS* 280:9 and r.19; cf. also below, [21].

3. W.G. Lambert, "A part of the ritual for the substitute king", *AfO* 18 (1957–58) 109–112; additions, *AfO* 19 (1959–60), 119. The extant copies come from the library of Assurbanipal, but the text itself was certainly composed much earlier, probably in the Kassite period or under the Isin II dynasty (at the latest). The existence of the Hittite rituals [4] even suggests an OB prototype.

4. H.M. Kümmel, *Ersatzrituale für den hethitischen König* (StBoT 3 [1967]). The texts published in this book date from about 1350–1250 B.C., see Kümmel p. 188. Their Babylonian origin is put beyond all doubt by the Akkadograms *PU-UḪ-ŠU/ŠÚ* and *LÚ PU-ḪIŠU* used for writing the Hittite word for the substitute king, as well as by several other Mesopotamian features and ritual termini (e.g. *LÚ A-ŠI-PI* "exorcist" and *MÁŠ.ḪUL.DÚB.BA.ḪI.A* "scapegoat") occurring in the texts.

5. ND 3484 (D.J. Wiseman, *Iraq* 15 pl.15): Administrative text mentioning a substitute king (MAN! *pu-ḫi*, coll. J.W. Kinnier Wilson, *CTN* 1 p. 111) in Rev. 11. The tablet, which comes from an archive dating to the reign of Adad-nērārī III, appears to contain an eponym date in r.9f: *lim-mu* TA DI x / ˡ.ᵈMAŠ-MAN-PAP "eponymy ... Ninurta-šarru-uṣur". This date presents serious problems. Since there was no such eponym as Ninurta-šarru-uṣur in the reign of Adad-nērārī or even his successor Shalmaneser IV, the sign MAŠ must be miscopied for either PA or ŠÚ, which would both yield acceptable eponyms, Nabû-šarru-uṣur (786 B.C.) and Marduk-šarru-uṣur (784 B.C.). The problem is that there were no eclipses calling for a substitute, and consequently no substitute king, in either year. Accordingly, the date

possibly represents an *urki* date, and should be amended to read *lim-mu ša*! *ur*!-*ki* or EGIR) ᴸᵈPA/ŠÚ-MAN-PAP. This would date the text to either 785 or 783 B.C. However, there were no really suitable eclipses in these years either. In 785 B.C., there were only the solar eclipse of August 16, during which Jupiter was not visible (but which might not have been observed in Mesopotamia since it started only 15 minutes before sunset), and a lunar one on August 30, during which Jupiter was clearly visible all the time; and in 783 B.C., no eclipses at all took place. This state of affairs prevents a reliable dating of the document for the time being. In addition to the problems already mentioned, one has also to take into consideration the fact that the order of eponyms in the last years of Adad-nērārī III is far from assured (cf. Gurney, *AnSt* 3 21). Moreover, there is the possibility that all the eponym dates in question have to be lowered by a year; see below, [6]. In any case, the principles followed in the Sargonid period would only have called for the enthronement of a substitute in 782 and (possibly) in 785 BC.

    a. ND 10026 (J.M. Kinnier Wilson, *CTN* 1 p. 111 and pl. 45f.): Text recording the issue of wine (from palace wine-cellars) in the eponym year of [ ]-šarru-uṣur (GEŠTINᴹᴱˢ KÚ ⌈ša⌉ [*lim-me* ᴸᵈDN]-MAN-PAP, Obv.1). The reverse pertains to the substitute king (MAN *pu-ḫi*, lines 12, 14 and 16): 1 homer 7 seahs issued to (*pānāt*) the substitute king in the centre of the city, for two [. . . .]; 5 homers 1 seah 5 liters in the city of Ubasê, issued to the substitute king, for two journeys; 14 homers 5 seahs in the Armory (*ekal māšarti*); in all 21 homers 3 seahs 5 liters for the substitute king. The total amount of wine consumed is almost exactly 10 times more than the amount consumed by the court of the substitute king in a day according to [6a]. This may imply that the reign of the substitute in this case lasted for about ten days (of which only the first one was spent in the royal palace in the center of Calah). If so, the reign in question cannot be identical with the one attested in [6] and [6a], and should accordingly (along with [5]) be dated to 785 B.C.

6. ND 3483 (D.J. Wiseman, *Iraq* 15 pl. 15): Text recording issues of victuals to the (court of the) substitute king (LUGAL *pu-ḫi*, lines 3, 5, 7 and 14) from the 22nd to the 24th of Du'ūzu, eponym year of Ninurta-nāṣir (ᴸᵈMAŠ!-PAP-*ir*), i.e. 783 BC. However, there were

no eclipses in that year. On the other hand, a substitute king must have been enthroned on account of the total lunar eclipse of June 1 (Simānu 14/15), -781, during which Jupiter was not visible. This creates a problem for the Assyrian chronology. Are all the dates in the early 8th century to be lowered by one year?

   a. ND 6213 + 6227 (J.W. Kinnier Wilson, *CTN* 1 No. 33, pl. 14f.): Text detailing rations of wine issued to the court of the substitute king (MAN *pu-ḫi*) Ābu 22 (year not specified), in all 2 homers 1 seah and 8 liters, or about 10% of the daily wine consumption of the royal court. Accepting tentatively Kinnier Wilson's hypothesis that the standard daily ration of wine per person was one cup of ca. 0.2 l, the court of the substitute king would have comprised about 320 persons, most of whom (100) would have been bodyguards *ša qurbūti*, Obv. 4), the rest consisting of lackeys, charioteers, musicians, bakers, confectioners, and the staff of the palace superintendent. One important magnate is mentioned in Col. ii4 as recipient of wine rations: Ṣilli-Ištar, the eponym of 787 BC. This same man also figures in *CTN* 1 No. 4, dating from 780 BC. Since the date mentioned in the heading (Ābu 22) is only a month later than the one mentioned in ND 3483 [6], it is extremely likely that both texts pertain to the same substitute king. The reign of this substitute (which started on June 1 = Simānu 14/15, 782 BC) would accordingly have lasted for at least 67 days.

7. *LAS* 30–32: Letters pertaining to a substitute king enthroned in Nineveh following the lunar eclipse of June 1, -678, or the lunar eclipse of September 3, -673, and re-enthroned 50 days later in Babylonia. See, in detail, commentary to *LAS* 30 and Addenda, p. 516.

8. *LAS* 136:12: Passage referring to a substitute king enthroned on account of the lunar eclipse of November 3, -676.

9. *LAS* 26f, 249, 278 and 292: Letters pertaining to a substitute king enthroned in Nineveh following the total lunar eclipse of July 2, -670, re-enthroned in Akkad 50 days later, and put to death after a 100-day reign. Two other letters, *LAS* 134 and *CT* 53 206, may also pertain to this case. Cf. *CT* 53 206:3'f ([ina ᵁᴿᵁ]URI [*e-ta-rab*] ⌜*i*⌝-*t*[*u*]-*ši-bi*) with *LAS* 279:10 (*a-na* ᵁᴿᵁ*Ak-kad e-ta-rab it-tu-ši-ib*) and 298:8 (*ina ŠÀ* ᵁᴿᵁ*Ak-kad-di it-tu-šib*), and note also the end of the letter, which may be restored: *šum-mu be-*[*lí i-qab-bi ina*] É.GAL [...] "if my lo[rd]

(i.e., the farmer) [commands, ... in] the palace ... " (r4 f.). The rest of the letter deals with building activities in Akkad (^{URU}URI, Obv.5').

10. *LAS* 185, 279f, 232 and 317: Letters pertaining to a substitute king enthroned in Nineveh slightly before the total lunar eclipse of December 27, -670, transferred to Akkad and re-enthroned there 5 days later, and put to death in January/February, 670 BC. The identity of this substitute king is known: Damqî, the son of the "bishop" of Akkad (*LAS* 280:24).

11. *LAS* 25, 28, 77, 135ff, 166f, 234f, and 257: Letters pertaining to a substitute king enthroned in Nineveh on account of the solar eclipse of May 27, -668, and put to death after a "reign" of 47 days. This substitute king stayed in Nineveh for the whole of his reign.

12. *LAS* 298f. and 205: Letters pertaining to a short (20-day) reign of a substitute king in the city of Akkad three months after the lunar eclipse of April 10, -665. This eclipse would not have called for a substitute king, for the planet Jupiter was visible during the eclipse. See commentary on *LAS* 298.

13. *LAS* 334: Letter addressed to the "farmer" in early May, 657 BC, and thus indirectly attesting to the enthronement of a substitute king on account of the solar eclipse of April 15, -656.

14. Herodotus, *Hist.* VII 15 and 17: Then Xerxes, greatly frightened at the vision, sprang from his couch, and sent a messenger to call Artabanus, who came at the summons, when Xerxes spoke to him in these words: "Artabanus, ... ever since I repented and changed my mind a dream has haunted me, which disapproves my intentions and has just gone from me with threats ["Know that unless you go forth to the war, this thing shall happen to you—as you are grown mighty and puissant in a short space, so likewise shall you within a little time be brought low indeed."] Now if this dream is sent to me from god, and if it is indeed his will that our troops should march against Greece, you too will have the same dream come to you and receive the same commands as myself. And this will be most sure to happen, I think, *if you put on the dress which I wear*, and then, after *taking your seat upon my throne*, lie down to sleep on my bed." ... Artabanus, thinking to show Xerxes that his words were naught, obeyed his orders. Having put on the garments which Xerxes was wont to wear, and, taken his seat upon the royal throne, he lay down to sleep upon the king's own bed. As

he slept, there appeared to him the very same dream which had been seen by Xerxes; it came and stood over Artabanus, and said: "So you are the man who, as if concerned for Xerxes, seeks to dissuade him from leading his armies against the Greeks! *But you shall not escape, either now or in time to come, because you sought to prevent that which is fated to happen.* As for Xerxes, it has been plainly told to himself what will befall him, if he refuses to perform my bidding." In such words the vision threatened him, and then endeavored to burn out his eyes with red-hot irons ... This is properly speaking not an instance of the substitute king ritual, but it contains all the essential elements of it: A divine message threatening the king, the magical transfer of the king's person upon another individual by robing and enthronement rites, and the irrevocability of the fate decreed by the gods both for the king and the substitute. If Herodotus heard this anecdote from Persian informants, it would certainly imply that the substitute king ritual was regularly practiced in the court of Xerxes (486–465 BC).

15. Plutarch (d. A.D. 120), *Lives*, Alexander LXXIII-IV: As he was upon his way to Babylon, Nearchus ... came to tell him he had met with some *Chaldean diviners*, who had *warned* him against Alexander's going thither. Alexander, however, took no thought of it, and went on, and when he came near the walls of the place, he saw a great many crows fighting with one another, some of whom fell down just by him ... Besides this, he was disturbed by many other prodigies ... And one day after he had undressed himself to be anointed, and was playing at ball, just as they were going to bring his clothes again, the young men who played with him perceived a *man clad in the king's robes with a diadem upon his head, sitting silently upon his throne.* They asked him who he was, to which he gave no answer a good while, till at last coming to himself he told them his name was Dionysius, that he was of Messenia, that for some crime of which he was accused he was brought thither from the seaside, and had been kept long in prison, that Serapis appeared to him, had freed him from his chains, conducted him to that place, and *commanded him to put on the king's robe and diadem, and to sit where they found him, and to say nothing.* Alexander, when he heard this, *by the direction of his soothsayers put the fellow to death,* but he lost his spirit, and grew diffident of the protection and assistance of the gods, and suspicious of his friends ... When once Alexander had given way to fears of supernatural

influence, his mind grew so disturbed and so easily alarmed that, if the least unusual or extraordinary thing happened, he thought it a prodigy or a presage, and *his court was thronged with diviners and priests whose business was to sacrifice and purify and foretell the future.* This episode, which took place shortly before Alexander's death in June, 323 BC, was recognized to pertain to the substitute king rites by Th. Jacobsen, ZA 52 (1957) 139[115], and indubitably gives a reliable account of the events. As noted by Kümmel [4], it is also told by two other Greek historians:

a. Arrian (died ca. AD 170), *Anabasis of Alexander*, VII 24: But Alexander's own end was now near. Aristobulos [contemporary of Alexander] says that the following occurrence was a prognostication of what was about to happen. He was distributing the army which had come with Peucestas from Persia ... and becoming thirsty he retired from his seat and thus left the royal throne empty. On each side of the throne were couches with silver feet, upon which his personal Companions were sitting. A certain man of obscure condition (some say that he was even one of the men kept under guard without being in chains), seeing the throne and the couches empty, ... walked through the line of eunuchs, ascended the throne, and sat down upon it. According to a Persian law, they did not make him rise from the throne, but rent their garments and beat their breasts and faces as if on account of a great wail. When Alexander was informed of this, he ordered the man who had sat upon his throne to be put to the torture, with the view of discovering whether he had done this according to a plan concerted by a conspiracy. But the man confessed nothing, except that it came into his mind at the time to act thus. Even more for this reason the *diviners* explained that this occurrence boded no good to him.

b. Diodorus Siculus (died ca. 20 B.C.), *Library of Universal History*, XVII 116: As the king was having himself anointed and the royal garment and the diadem were lying on a couch beside the throne, a native prisoner freed himself from his chains and, unnoticed by the guards, made his way through the doors into the hall without anybody trying to stop him. He went to the throne, dressed in royal robes, put on the diadem, sat upon the throne and remained quiet. When the incident was noticed, the king, though frightened by it, went to the throne and, concealing his fright, calmly asked the man who he was and for what purpose he had done it. As he answered that he was aware of no reason whatsoever, the king consulted the soothsayers about the omen and then, by their direction, put the man to death so as to make the unlucky portents turn against him. Himself, he dressed again in his robes and sacrificed to the protective gods, but felt restless. He remembered the prophecy of the Chaldeans and castigated the philosophers who had persuaded him to enter Babylon, admiring the skill of the Chaldeans and their vision . . .

16. Dio Chrysostomus (died ca. A.D. 115), *De Regno*, IV 66–68: "You, too", continued Diogenes, "have a fiery temperament, the same kind of a dangerous and violent sting. Why don't you throw away what you are now wearing, put on a simple smock-frock and serve those who conduct themselves better as rulers, instead of running about with that ridiculous diadem? Or are you perhaps planning next to grow a comb and a tiara like a cock? Don't you know the Sakaia rites performed by the Persians, against whom you are now planning to march?" Alexander immediately asked what kind of a ceremony that was, for he wanted to learn everything about the Persians. "*They take a prisoner condemned to death, seat him upon the throne of the king, robe him in royal garments and let him issue orders, drink and revel, yes, during those days he is even allowed to amuse himself with the king's concubines, and nobody prevents him from doing what he wants. Then, however, he is dragged out, whipped, and hanged.*" What do you think this festival stands for? And why do the Persians celebrate it? Isn't the idea as follows: the power and title of the king is often grabbed by stupid and vicious men, who for a while indulge in revelries and soon find an infamous end. Therefore, it also is natural that the ignorant fool rejoices and congratulates himself when freed from his chains, but the one who knows laments bitterly, resists being taken along, and would much rather remain in chains as before. You, too, fool, don't try to be a king before you have got reason! Until then it is better to give no commands but live a life of one's own in a smock-frock." The origin of this anecdote is unknown, but it certainly represents a tradition not dependent on the following one.

17. Athenaios Naucratica (ca. A.D. 230), *Deipnosophistai*, XIV 639c (fragm. 16M): "In the first book of the Babyloniaka, Berossus tells that from the sixteenth day of the month Loos there went on for five days in Babylon a festival called the Sakaia, during which it was customary that masters were given commands by servants, one of whom was led out of his house clad in robes resembling those of the king, and he says that this one was called Zoganes. The said festival is also mentioned by Ctesias in the second book of his Persika." This passage probably refers to the Babylonian New Year's festival and has (despite the name Sakaia which it shares with the preceding entry) nothing to do with the substitute king ritual.

18. Suetonius (died A.D. 150), *Vitae*, Claudius XXIX 3: "But it is beyond all belief, that at the marriage which Messalina had contracted with her paramour Silius he [Claudius] signed the contract for the dowry with his hand, being induced to do so on the ground that the marriage was a feigned one, designed *to avert and turn upon another a danger which was inferred from certain portents to threaten the emperor himself*. Cf. XXVI 2: But when he learned that besides other shameful and wicked deeds she had actually married Gaius Silius, and that a formal contract had been signed in the presence of witnesses, he put her to death." That this garbled account may attest to the ritual of the substitute king practiced in the court of Claudius (A.D. 41–54) was pointed out by C.J. Gadd, *AfO* 18 (1957–58), 218. By marrying the empress Messalina, Silius had conveniently become a *substitute emperor*.

19. John Malcolm, *History of Persia*, Vol. I (London 1829), p. 346: "While engaged in preventing the inroads of the Usbegs ... he (= Abbas the Great) was suddenly called from all considerations of foreign or domestic policy, by *a prediction of his astrologers; who, from the aspect of the heavenly bodies, had discovered that a most serious danger impended over the sovereign of Persia*. Abbas was not exempt from the superstition of the age in which he lived, and did not hesitate to adopt the strange expedient by which his counsellors proposed to avert the dreaded omen. *He abdicated the throne*; and a person of the name of Yusoofee, whom Persian authors take care to tell us was *an unbeliever* (probably a Christian), *was crowned*; and for three days, if we are to believe these historians [Zubd-ul-Tuarikh], *he enjoyed not only the name and state, but the power of the king*. The cruel farce ended as was to be expected. Yusoofee *was put to death; the decree of the stars was fulfilled by this*

sacrifice; and Abbas, who reascended his throne in a most propitious hour, was promised by his astrologers a long and glorious reign." This incident took place in 1591 (A.H. 1000), less than 300 years ago!

20. E.W. Lane, *The Arabian Nights* (London 1889), Vol. 2, p. 312 ff: The Story of Abu-l-Ḥasan the Wag, or the Sleeper Awakened. Even though this story, placed in the reign of Harun ar-Rashid, unlike the substitute king ritual has a happy end, it can hardly be doubted that it has been inspired by the ritual.

21. A.H. Layard, *Nineveh and Its Remains* (London 1849), p. 271: "When Keritli Oglu, Mohammed Pasha, first came to Mosul, this sect [the Yezidis] was amongst the objects of his cupidity and tyranny. He seized by treachery, as he supposed, their head or high priest; but Sheikh Nasr had time to *escape the plot against him, and to substitute in his place* the second in authority, who was carried as prisoner to the town. Such is the attachment shown by the Yezidis to their chief that the deceit was not revealed, and *the substitute bore with resignation* the tortures and imprisonment inflicted upon him." While this episode has nothing to do with the substitute king ritual as such, it does illustrate the mental climate that fostered the performance of the rite in the Near East from the earliest times on, and furnishes a living example of what the letter formula cited under [2] could have meant in practice.

Chapter 8

Letters from Assyrian Scholars

THIS CHAPTER INCLUDES THE portions of letters to Assyrian kings that pertain to Assyrian substitutes, along with comments on substitution. Scholars who seek greater depth should consult the full original publication of the letters.

Letters from Assyrian Scholars to the Kings Esarhaddon and Assurbanipal

(by Simo Parpola)

LAS Letter 25

Addressee: "Farmer" Esarhaddon

Date: June 9, 669 BCE

Text: To the "farmer", my lord, (from) your servant Ištar-šumu-ēreš: Good health to the farmer, my lord! May the gods Nabû and Marduk bless the farmer, my lord. As regards the wa[tc]h (for the lunar eclipse) about which the [farmer], my [lord], wrot[e to m]e: "[....] (*long break*) "If it should occ[ur], what is the word about it?" The 14th day (signifies) the Eastland, month Simānu (signifies) the Westland, (and) the relevant "decision" (pertains) to Ur. And if it occurs, the region it afflicts and the wind blowing will be excerpted as well.

Comments: ... "I shall send the king, my lord, a definite report as to whether it (the eclipse) takes place or not" ... information concerning the eclipse could be given even before the event had actually occurred. ...

Notes: r7'. *kaqquru* "area, region" was the technical term for "moon quadrant" ...; in the eclipse of June 10, 669, only the quadrant of Subartu/Assyria was eclipsed. ...

LAS Letter 26

Addressee: Esarhaddon

Date: September 5, 671 BCE

Text: To my lord, (from) your servant Ištar-šumu-ēreš: Good health to my lord! May the gods Nabû and Marduk bless you my lord. As regards the substitute king [about whom] my lord wrote to me: "[...] emerges from the flank [of ...]" (*long break*) [As regards(?) the s]igns [about which my lord w]rote to me, [after] we had enthroned him, we let him hear (them) in front of the Sun god. Also yesterday I let him hear (them), *cut off*(?) *and bound close to him*. Now I shall do again as my lord wrote to me. (*Rest of obverse broken away*)

Comments: ... But it is known that on three occasions, following the total lunar eclipses of September 674, July 671 and December 671, the substitute king initially enthroned in Nineveh was taken to Babylonia and re-enthroned there (see LAS 30, 134, 249, 279 and 292.)[48] In the last case the re-enthronement followed very soon after the initial enthronement (*LAS* 280); the date of the other re-enthronements is unknown, yet it would be logical to assume that the substitute king, under normal conditions, spent half his reign in Nineveh and the other half in Akkad. Thus the three re-enthronements in question would have occurred respectively about October 23, 674, August 21, 671, and January 1, 670. The middlemost date fits perfectly, whereas the other two fail completely ... the substitute king was resident in Akkad in fall 671. By contrast, as already stated, no other known enthronement of the substitute king provides an explanation for Obv. 89. The dating to 671 is finally also supported by the fact that the king is in the present letter addressed not as "Farmer", as in *LAS* 25 (669 BC) and 31 (674 BC), but merely as "my lord".⁴⁹

Notes: r1'ff. See discussion sub *LAS* 27. On the practice of having the substitute king "take on himself" all the bad omens threatening the safety of the king even at his re-enthronement, see in more detail *LAS* 279:11 ff. and 30:6 ff. r8'. Cancel the translation of this line in Pt. 1 and render: "I attached (them) to his seam". While the meaning of *ag-da-da-ad* in the preceding line remains uncertain, the idea of the passage is clear: the evil omens previously recited to the substitute king were written down (on papyrus or pergament scroll, or a perforated cuneiform tablet) and attached to the garment of the substitute, to make sure that he was constantly "afflicted" by them....⁴⁸

In only one case (*LAS* 279) is it explicitly stated that the substitute king enthroned in Nineveh was the same as the one enthroned in Akkad. But since Esarhaddon was king of both Assyria and Babylonia, it was obligatory that one man only functioned as his substitute in both countries in the other case, too.⁴⁹

This form of address is, it is true, also used in *LAS* 28. But in that case, the title "Farmer" could not be used anyway, since the substitute king had not yet been enthroned and the king thus had not yet changed status, whereas in the present case no such obstacle was in the way.

LAS Letter 27

Addressee: "Farmer" Esarhaddon

Date: August 21, 671 BCE

Text: [To the "farmer"], my [lord], (from) [your servant Ištar-šumu-ēreš: [Good health to] my lord! [May the gods Nabû and] Marduk bless you [my lord]. [What my lord wr]ote to me: "[Let him hear the signs] in front of the [Sun] god! [.....] soon [.....] I saw [.... wh]at ever I have not seen [...] is known to my lord (*remainder lost*).

Comments: The omission of the word "Farmer" ... indicate[s] that this fragment is approximately contemporaneous with *LAS* 26 ..., where the writer asks the king to communicate to him all the evil omens he is possibly aware of, shows that the letter was written at the time of the re-enthronement of the substitute king in question. The grounds for dating this re-enthronement to Ulūlu 4 = August 21, 671, are presented sub *LAS* 26. The temporal distance of the two letters would thus be about two weeks. This agrees well with the proposed dating, supposing that *LAS* 26 was written soon after the writer received the king's answer to the present letter. . . . journey from Nineveh to Akkad took normally about 5 days,[51] . . . it is probable that at the moment of enthronement he recited to the substitute king only whatever omens he was himself aware of, and later supplemented the inventory by the omens communicated in the king's letter.

Notes: [51]Cf. Rassam, *Asshur and the Land of Nimrod* (1897), p. 193, describing his journey from Baghdad to Mosul, which he accomplished in six days on horseback: "As I wished to proceed as fast as I could, I chose the *quickest* mode of travelling, though not the easiest, in having recourse to the Government postal service, by which means I was enabled to make long stages at a quick pace, partly galloping, and partly trotting. At each station we changed horses and escort. Though the distance from Baghdad to Mosul via Karkook and Arweel (the ancient Arbela) is only one hundred hours, or three hundred miles, I accomplished it in six days, allowing a good margin for detentions and necessary night rest. Some part of the road was rather muddy and difficult to ride through, in consequence of the frost and the heavy rains that fell during the winter."

LAS Letter 28

Addressee: "Farmer" Esarhaddon

Date: May 27, 669 BCE

Text: [To the "farmer"], our lord], (from) [your servants] Ištar-šumu-ēreš, [Urad]-Ea, (and) [Marduk]-šākin-šumi: The best [of he]alth [to] our lord! [May the gods Nabû and] Marduk bless our lord. [What] our lord [wr]ote to us: [If, on the 30]th day, a solar [eclipse takes] place, we shall [p]erform the pertinent [apotropaic ritual; somebody should s]it (on the throne) [and remo]ve [your evil].

Comments:

Date: Ajāru 29, eponymy of Šamaš-kāšid-ajābi = May 27, 669 BC . . . there were only three solar eclipses visible in Nineveh between 680-663 BC, viz. those of June 17, -678; May 27, -668; and August 28, -663. The first possibility can be ruled out since Ištar-šumu-ēreš heads the writer team of the letter (see sub *LAS* 31); the last is extremely improbable as no other letter of the present corpus is datable to 664 BC. . . .

Notes: Cancel the restoration . . .; since the substitute king had not yet been enthroned (r4), the king was certainly called simply "lord" (as in *LAS* 26-27) . . . 12. . . . restore [*ma-a* UD 29].KÁM*, and translate: "A solar [eclipse occur*red* on the 29]th".

LAS Letter 30

Addressee: "Farmer" Esarhaddon

Date: October 23, 674 BCE

Text: To the "farmer", my lord, (from) your servant Nabû-zēru-līšer: Good health to my lord! May the gods Nabû and Marduk bless my lord many years. I wrote down whatever signs there were, be they celestial, terrestrial or of malformed births, (and) had them recited in front of the Sun god, one after the other. They were treated with wine, washed with water (and) anointed with oil; I had those birds cooked (and) made them eat them. The substitute king of the land of Akkad took the signs on himself. He cried: "Because of what bad sign have you enthroned a substitute king?" And he speaks: "Say [in] the presence of the farmer: in [. . .] win[e . . . .]

Comments: No solar eclipses were observable in Mesopotamia between 678 and 670 BC . . . ; the eclipse in question was consequently lunar. The fact that a substitute king was needed for Babylonia implies that the right side of the moon had been eclipsed, and in addition, that the planet Jupiter had not been visible during the eclipse . . . These two requirements are met by only one lunar eclipse between 680 and 672 BC, that of September 3, -673 . . . This was a total eclipse and so required the enthronement of a substitute king not only in Akkad but in Nineveh, too; and in the reign of Esarhaddon who at the same time was king of both Assyria and Babylonia, the practice was that the same substitute functioned as the king of both countries, residing the first half of his 100-day reign in Nineveh and the last half in Akkad . . . The present letter would consequently pertain to recoronation ceremonies in Akkad 50 days after the occurrence of the said eclipse, i.e. on October 23 ... 674 BC. This date fits perfectly all data of the letter. Firstly, it explains the curious outcry of the substitute king ...: since the day of the coronation was 50 days removed from the eclipse, there was – contrary to his previous coronation immediately preceded by a shattering omen visible to everybody – no apparent motivation for the ceremony. Secondly, the very fact that the substitute wondered at his transfer to Akkad indicates that the case had no precedents in recent memory and thus implies that the lunar eclipse in question was the first total one in Esarhaddon's reign requiring the enthronement of a substitute king. ...

Notes: 10f ... The persons intended are, of course, the substitute king and his queen.

11f. *"I made them eat those birds"*; this measure can hardly have been part of the coronation ceremonies which must have reached their climax at the anointment of the substitute and his wife ... "he crowned him king", lit. "he put oil on his head"..., and therefore in all probability belonged to the rites performed in order to have the substitute "take on himself" the omens threatening the safety of the king. The birds in question were, accordingly, presumably ominous (or had been involved in an ominous incident; cf., e.g., Plutarch, *Lives* VII, Alexander LLXXIII: "Certain Chaldeans had met him and advised that Alexander should keep away from Babylon. Alexander paid no heed to this, but continued on his march; and when he was arrived at the walls, he saw many ravens flying about and clawing one another, and some fell dead at his feet" – an omen immediately preceding the enthronement of a substitute king); by having the substitutes literally *eat* them, the persons in charge of the ceremonies probably wanted to make sure that the evil of the birds would irrevocably and concretely attach to the substitute king and his queen instead of the true king and his wife. Cf. note on 26 r.8'.

14. ... *"The substitute king cried out"*: surely an exceptional incident; the substitute kings were expected to keep their mouths shut while exercising their duty (cf. "a man clad in the king's robes with a diadem upon his head sitting silently upon his throne ... asked who he was ... gave no answer", Plutarch, loc. cit.; "sat upon the throne and remained quiet", Diodorus XVII 116.

17. *"And he spoke"*: That a man forced to die for the king still remains so loyal to his lord as to voluntarily expose to him a conspiracy which, if allowed to mature, might have saved his life, may seem strange to us but probably was more natural in the eyes of the contemporaries. Note that a similar mental attitude is still attested for Mesopotamia of the 19th century by Layard, *Nineveh and Its Remains I*, p. 271: "The substitute bore with resignation the tortures and imprisonment inflicted upon him . . ."

LAS Letter 31

Addressee: "Farmer" Esarhaddon

Date: September 3, 673 BCE

Text: [To] the "farmer", [our] lord, (from) your [servants] Nabû-zēru-līš[er], [Ad]ad-šumu-uṣur, Nabû-šumu-[iddina], [Urad]-Ea (and) Ištar-šumu-[ēreš]: [Good hea]lth to [our lo]rd! (*Remainder lost except for the last line* :) We [shall go] to Nineveh.

Comments: . . . the way in which the king is addressed can only imply that the letter was, at the same time, 1) a report of the occurrence of an alarming eclipse . . . an announcement that the collegium had immediately enthroned a substitute to eliminate the danger threatening the king; had the substitute not yet been enthroned, the king should have been addressed differently (cf. sub *LAS* 28). The eclipse in question can only be that of September 3, -673 . . . or an earlier eclipse during which Jupiter was not visible. . . . The odds are for the former alternative, considering that there is a gap of three years before one finds a suitable eclipse preceding September 674 (November 3, 677; cf. App. F1). The letter thus predates *LAS* 30 by about 50 days.

LAS Letter 77

Addressee: "Farmer," probably Esarhaddon

Date: June 10, 669 BCE

Text: To the "farmer", my lord, (from) your servant Nabû-šumu-iddina, the foreman of the collegium of ten (scribes) of Nineveh: May the gods Nabû (and) Marduk bless the farmer, my lord. On the 14th day we were watching the Moon: the Moon was eclipsed.

Comments:

Date: ... the fact that the letter is addressed to the "Farmer" implies that the eclipse concerned was preceded by a solar one. *LAS* 31 shows that Nabû-šumu-iddina was a contemporary of Nabû-zēru-līšer, Adad-šumu-uṣur, Ištar-šumu-ēreš and Urad-Ea; hence the present letter can with certainty be placed between 681 and 663 BC. ...

LAS Letter 134

Addressee: Esarhaddon

Date: 671 BCE

Text: To the king, my lord, (from) your servant Adad-šumu-uṣur: Good health to the king, my lord! May the gods Nabû (and) Marduk bless the king, my lord. As regards the substitute king of Akkad, order should be given to enthrone (him). As regards the clothes of the king, my lord, (and) the garments for the statue of the substitute king, as regards the necklace [of go]ld, the scepter (and) the throne (*break*) We shall remove [...] (and) enthrone [...]. Now they should give the orders; *soon after the reduction* we shall go. What is it that the king, my lord, says?

Comments:

Date: The reference to Akkad as the scene of the substitute king ritual dates this letter to 671 BC. ...

LAS Letter 135

Addressee: Esarhaddon

Date: July 6, 669 BCE

Text: To the king, [my lord], (from) your servant Adad-[šumu-uṣur]: Good health to the k[ing, my lord]! May the gods Nabû (and) Marduk bless the king, my lord. As regards the substitute king about whom the king, my lord, wrote to me: "How many days should he sit?" We waited for a solar eclipse, (but) the eclipse did not take place. Now, if the gods are seen in opposition on the 15th day, he could go to his fate on the 16th. Or if it suits the king, my lord, better, he could (as well) sit the full 100 days.

Comments: . . . full moon on the 16th of Du'ūzu would have portended imprisonment of the king of Assyria for a month . . . ; this explains the direction given here that the substitute king may go to his fate on the 16th, *if* the opposition already occurs on the 15th (a harmless omen); otherwise, his reign would certainly have been extended considerably.

LAS Letter 136

Addressee: Esarhaddon

Date: June 23, 669 BCE

Text: [To the king, my lord], (from) your servant Adad-šumu-uṣur: Good health to the king, my lord! May the gods Nabû (and) Marduk bless] the king, [my] lord. The charge [of the] re[ar palace is doing well]. [As regards the s]ubstitute [king] about whom the king, [my lord, wrote] to me: "I was told [that he should sit until the 2]6th of Ulūlu; *would it (then) be too soon if* we perform (the ritual) *Bīt salā'mê* in the month Tašrītu?", as the substitute king was sitting in the month Araḫsamna, in Simānu [. . . (*long break*) We are [n]ow [waiting for] a [solar] eclipse; [if] it will pass by, the king, my lord, should act in t[his way]. We will see [. . . (*remainder lost*).

Comments:

Notes: . . . 9. The date can be restored either as *Ulūlu* [2]6 or *Ulūlu* ⌜8⌝. In the latter case, the substitute king's reign would have been scheduled to continue exactly 100 days after his enthronement following the solar eclipse of Ajāru . . .; in the former, it would have been due to last an additional 100 days after the lunar eclipse, in all 115 days.

LAS Letter 139

Addressee: "Farmer" Esarhaddon

Date: June 5, 669 BCE (?)

Text: [To] the "farmer", our lord, (from) your [servants] Adad-šumu-uṣur and Marduk-šākin-šumi: Good health to our lord! May the gods Nabû (and) Marduk bless our lord.

As regards the girl about whom my lord said: "At what time should she come in?", since he is an "early bird", let the day (= the sun) rise for an hour and a half, thereupon she may enter. Soon after that my lord should have himself shaved. The ritual is on the evening of the 11th day.

Comments: ... since the letter is signed by two high-ranking exorcists and addressed to the "Farmer", it can with reason be supposed to deal with some phase of the substitute king ritual. Von Soden (1956) plausibly suggested that the "girl" referred to ... was the queen of the substitute king, referred to as "virgin" ... in the substitute king ritual tablet ... found here actually means "virgin" rather than "girl" ... Unfortunately, the fragmentary ritual tablet, in its present state of preservation, contains no more references to this "substitute queen", so one can only conjecture about the purpose of the visit alluded to in the present letter. Was the king perhaps expected to have sexual intercourse with the girl?

Notes: r6. ... The shaving ritual here mentioned probably had nothing to do with the earthquake Namburbi discussed under *LAS* 137; nevertheless, its purpose doubtless was likewise purificatory ... It seems evident that contact with the girl was considered contaminating, which supports the hypothesis that the queen of the substitute king indeed is in question. r8f. ... The letter was written either in Ābu 671 or Simānu-Du'ūzu 669, since in 666 the substitute king was enthroned (and remained resident) in *Akkad*, whereas in Kanūnu 671 he was moved to Akkad hardly 6 days after his enthronement in Nineveh on Kanūnu 14 ...

LAS Letter 166

Addressee: "Farmer" Esarhaddon

Date: July 8, 669 BCE

Text: To [the "farmer", our lord], (from) your servants [Adad-šumu-uṣur] and Marduk-šākin-šumi: [Good] health to our lord! [May the gods Nabû and] Marduk [bles]s our lord.

As regards the 15th day [about which our lord] said: The substitute [kin]g should [g]o to his destiny! I will perform my rite on the 16th day as before", the 16th is a good day to perform (the rite). As our fathers did to their lords, and (as) the farmer has done once and twice, (as) Bēl and Nabû have ordained, just like that will we do now. Why should we wait as if it were not fortunate? And just like the pupils have said: "In Enbu Bēl Arḫi it is recorded as a favorable day", just like that we shall keep it. Hence the 16th day is among the good days (and) is good, (but) the 17th day is not good.

Comments: ... the addressee had *at least* twice gone through a (purification) ritual following the execution of the substitute king. This proves, firstly, that the letter was addressed to Esarhaddon, and secondly, that it cannot have been written before 671 BC, since the substitute king ritual had been performed only twice before that year in Esarhaddon's reign. ... Within the time brackets 671-669 BC thus obtained, three different substitute kings were enthroned: one in Du'ūzu (July), 671, another in Kanūnu (December) of the same year, and a third in Ajāru (May), 669. The first of these reigned for 100 days and was put to death on Tašrītu 22 = October 7, 671, or a few days later (see. . . *LAS* 292) ... This letter, also by Adad-šumu-uṣur, refers to a watch for a solar eclipse and then goes on to suggest that the substitute king currently reigning may "go to his fate" on the 16th, *if* the full moon is observed on the 15th: alternatively, the substitute may complete his normal 100-day reign. That is exactly where the present letter begins: the king *endorses* the option of the 15th day ... , *tells* that the substitute has to be executed and *not* allowed to complete his reign ... and *affirms* he will perform his purificatory ritual on the 16th according to the established practice ...

Discussion: Leaving out of consideration the mini-reign reported in *LAS* 298, which was due to a misunderstanding on the king's part, the present letter provides the only certain attestation of a substitute king ritual terminated before its normal end; in all other cases ... the substitute obviously was allowed to "sit" full 100 days ... Accepting that the substitute began his reign on Ajāru 29, immediately after the solar eclipse, ... the ritual under consideration lasted only 47 days, i.e. not even half of its normal duration. Why? Two explanations seem possible. First, the king may have gotten *tired* of the *repeated* performance of the ritual in recent years, which certainly to some extent at least inconvenienced his life, and he may thus have wanted to finish the ritual as soon as possible. This is, however, improbable, knowing the psyche of Esarhaddon (cf. sub *LAS* 246); he must have been happy with all kind of protection and attention he could get. It is true that *LAS* 135:8ff and 134:9f clearly indicate that the king was getting impatient, but his impatience then was probably due to something else than just *boredom*. The beginning of the king's 12th year had been full of disappointments and frightening portents: cancellation of the return of Bēl to Babylon in mid-Ajāru (*LAS* 29), solar eclipse at the end of the same month (*LAS* 28 and 104); an ill-portending earthquake in the beginning of Simānu (*LAS* 35, 137 and 234), a lunar eclipse predicting evil to Assyria in the middle of the same month (*LAS* 25, *RMA* 271, etc.) and immediately after that, a sudden illness of a baby who apparently was very dear to the king (*LAS* 167, 152-156, 136 and 126). As a result of all this, he may have grown increasingly nervous and restless, unwilling to wait for months until the danger threatening him would be definitely eliminated; especially the last adversity, which was a decidedly personal one, may have given rise to a desire to get rid of the substitute as soon as possible (see on 136:11). That it was, in principle, possible to dethrone the substitute before his 100-day reign (cf. note on 135 r.6) was over cannot be doubted, even though no clear statement to this effect is extant in the substitute king ritual tablet: otherwise Adad-šumu-uṣur could hardly have given the king this option in *LAS* 135.

LAS Letter 179

Addressee: Esarhaddon

Date: July 669 BCE

Text: To the king, my lord, (from) your servants Marduk-šākin-šumi: Good health to the king, my lord! May the gods [Nabû] and Marduk bless the king, my lord. As regards the figurines to be buried about which the king, my lord, wrote to me, "Where will they be buried?", it is said in the (ritual) tablet as follows: "You bury [at the pal]ace ga[te]".

Now, if the king consents, [... *(long break)* Also tomorrow, after the king has gone out, they should bury in front of the main room and the bedrooms, and where the king instructs as well. Daytime or nighttime is indifferent; one may bury whenever one likes. I will bury (figurines) in like manner here.

Comments:

Discussion: As can be seen without much difficulty, this letter concerns the burying of prophylactic figurines (*timru*, see on Obv. 5) in various parts of the royal palace. The text contains too few details to make it possible to identify the ritual concerned with certainty, but it seems quite possible that the prophylactic ceremonies performed after the death of the substitute king ... are in question ...

Notes: 5. ... The substitute king ritual tablet prescribes (*AfO* 18 110 f) the burying of the following items: two raging dogs at [outer] gate ...; two bulls of Šamaš at *papāḫu* chapel; two hydras at palace gate; two capricorns at bedroom ...; two kneeling figures in the middle of palace courtyard; and two lion-men at side entrance. r3f. ... "On the 5th, when the king goes out of doors, an exorcist should move a censer (and) a torch past (the king)." Does the present passage refer to the same situation? The seemingly incidental remark about the king's exit from the palace may imply that he had previously not been permitted to leave the palace precincts for safety reasons; this would support the hypothesis that the letter pertains to the final phase of a substitute king ritual.

LAS Letter 185

Addressee: Esarhaddon

Date: December 25, 671 BCE

Text: [To] the king, [my] lord, (from) [your servant] Marduk-šākin-šumi: [Good he]alth to the king, my lord! May the gods [Nabû and] Marduk bless the king, my lord.

    3 "hand-lifting prayers to be recited before the god [Nusku],
    3 "before the Moon-god, 3 before the constellation [Pleiades],
    2 "before the star Sirius,
    2 "b[efo]re the planet Ma[rs],

2 "b[efore the st]ar V[ega],
2 "be[fore the st]ar [....],
1 "be[fore the st]ar [....],
1 "bef[ore the star ....],

the incantation (beginning) "Ea, [Šamaš and Assalluḫi]" belonging to the apotropaic ritual against all kinds of evil, as the apotropaic ritual (called) "If the Moon and the Sun have become *a grievance* to the noble and his country":

(these) tablets, totaling to 21, I have today performed on the river bank; Urad-Ea will perform (his share) on the roof of the palace tonight. (As) the king, my lord, knows, an exorcist has to avoid reciting a "hand-lifting" prayer on an evil day: (therefore) I shall now look up, collect (and copy numerous - 20 to 30 - canonical and non-canonical tablets, (but) perform (the prayers) (only) tomorrow evening (and) on the night of the 15th day. On the 16th (and) 17th I shall perform those before the goddesses Venus, Ninlil, Zarpānītu, Tašmētu, Gula (and) Nanâ as well. I have opened my fists (and) prayed to the gods: all is well, the gods have blessed the king, my lord, and his sons. True, if it suits the king, my lord, word should be sent to Calah (and) the "hand-lifting" prayers before the Moon-god as well as the apotropaic ritual against evil of all kind should be performed for the crown prince and the prince of Babylon. What's wrong (with it)?

I have also been pondering about the impending observation of the Moon; let this be [my] advice. If it is convenient, let us put somebody on the throne. The night [of the 15th day] will come, (and) he will be afflicted [during it]; but he *will sa*[*ve* (?) *your life* (?)] I am listening - [the king, my lord], knows the Babylonians (and) what [rebe]lious plans they [con]ceive. (These) plotters should be af[flicted]! Tomorrow - if it seems good - I shall come to the audience and speak to the king.

Comments:

Date: In Rev. 14 ff the writer refers to an unspecified but alarming lunar observation, on account of which he proposes that a substitute (king) should be put on the throne; this substitute would be "afflicted" *on the night* of the [th] day.

On the basis of these data it is easy to prove that the letter was written approximately a day before an expected lunar eclipse: the performance of the prayers, incantation and apotropaic ritual mentioned at the beginning of the letter presupposes a lunar eclipse which, however, could not yet have occurred since the letter was written only on the 13th day and since the substitute was to be "afflicted" only on a *coming* night. That the "observation" (*tāmartu*) of the moon actually refers to this eclipse is clear from the fact that it was to be made in the nighttime and in the middle of the month. The apotropaic ritual concerning both the sun and the moon was accordingly intended to counteract the "evil" of the (ill-portending) opposition of the two bodies.

Secondly, it is virtually certain that the eclipse in question had been predicted for the 15th day. The substitute king was scheduled to be enthroned before the eclipse actually took place . . . ; but when the chief exorcist was to *discuss* the matter with the king, the night of the 14th day had already passed! Hence the eclipse concerned can have occurred on the 15th *at the earliest* and on the 16th at the latest; the later date is only possible supposing a calendrical error.

Thirdly, the surety with which the eclipse could be predicted (the performance of the *Bīt rimki* ritual had already begun and enthronement of a substitute king was seriously considered) strongly suggests that the eclipse was TOTAL . . .

Discussion: . . . The information about the *substitute king ritual* is perhaps even more significant. It appears that the proposal to enthrone a substitute unambiguously originated, at least in the present case, with the chief exorcist Marduk-šākin-šumi (not with the king) and that the substitute was seated on the throne, if possible, already *before* the eclipse had taken place. . . .

Notes: r13. . . . The implication seems to be that while the *bīt rimki* ritual was supposed to protect the king and his "house", the two crown princes (who were not resident at court) *possibly* constituted a special case and therefore needed additional protection.

r18. Certainly referring to the enthronement of a substitute king. . . . "when we enthroned him" (lit. "made him, . . . the substitute king, sit") . . . "what is the bad omen on account of which you have enthroned a substitute king?" . . . "they should give order to enthrone (a substitute)" . . . "why did they enthrone (him) in Akkad?" The corresponding G-stem "to sit" (. . . on the throne) is used quite similarly: . . . "how many days should he (the substitute king) sit on the throne?" . . . "the [substitute] king who was seated on the throne in Nineveh on the 15th day" ... "he should sit on the throne for a 100 days", ... this "technical" use of *wšb* (in the meaning "*to sit on the throne*") was confined to texts dealing with the substitute king ritual; in all other contexts the verb required in this meaning a specification like *ina kussê*, or the like.

r25. ... The implication of the passage clearly is that the prospective substitute king should be chosen from among Babylonians fomenting rebellious (separistic) or criminal plans; the writer probably had in mind Babylonian noblemen or their sons held as hostages in Nineveh (cf. Parpola, *Iraq* 34 [1972] 33f). The suggestion did not necessarily have any political aims ...; it was apparently an established practice to choose the substitute from among criminals ... In any case, the ultimate choice fell on a politically significant person: Damqî, the son of the bishop (*šatammu*) of Akkad, whose eventual death badly upset the inhabitants of Akkad. See *LAS* 279 and 280.

LAS Letter 205

Addressee: Esarhaddon

Date: July 666 BCE

Text: To the king, my lord, (from) your servant Nabû-nādin-šumi: Good health to the king, my lord! May the gods Nabû and Marduk bless the king, my lord. As regards what the king, my lord, said to me: "Discuss (it) with Balasî", I have (now) done (so). He said as follows: "He should sit down (on the throne) on the 15th (and) get up on the 22nd; on the 24th day the king should go down to the river (and) perform his ritual." He also said: "Let us talk (about this) to the king (himself), the king should hear what we have to say." He and I should (now) have an audience with the king; we shall instruct the king, our lord, how the ritual will be performed. It is a complicated one, (and) it would be advantageous if the king would listen to what we have to say. As regards the malformed birth about which the king wrote to me: "It is crippled", I have written to the king as it is written on the tablet.

Comments:

Discussion: The identification of the rites alluded to in this letter poses a problem. While the writer refers to a ritual (to undo the evil) of a malformed birth (*šá iz-bi*) in Rev. 9, and while the *izbu* namburbi (Ebeling, *RA* 50 86ff and dupls.) involved, among other things, a trip to the river bank by the man affected by the evil, as also prescribed in Obv. 11f of the present letter, this namburbi does not qualify for the ritual described on the Obverse: the wording of Rev. 9 ff clearly indicates that the topic of the *izbu* ritual is there introduced for the first time, and analysis of the *izbu* namburbi shows that its structure and ritual components entirely differ from the scenario outlined in the present letter. . . . the letter concerned the enthronement and dethronement of a substitute king . . . and subsequent purification rites to be undergone by the king . . . the proposed reign of the substitute king would have been exceptionally short, only 7 days (15th through 22nd), the normal duration being 100 days . . . While there is evidence that the "reign" was occasionally terminated before the full 100 days had elapsed (see under *LAS* 166 and 280), even the shortest reign so far attested lasted for 20 days . . . , and that reign was explicitly characterized as exceptional in every respect. . . . The proposed day of enthronement, [Du'ūzu] 15, would then have been the 88th day after the lunar eclipse of Nisannu, which furnished the cause of the ritual, and the proposed dethronement would have taken place 95 days after the same eclipse.

Notes: 7. . . . reference . . . lends support to the hypothesis that the letter deals with the substitute king ritual, since proposals to enthrone a substitute appear often to have been made by collegiums of scholars including a scribe and an exorcist (cf. *LAS* 28 and 31). 11 f. . . . Note that the king was supposed to undergo a purification ritual on the day following the dethronement of the substitute king (*LAS* 166), just as implied by the present passage.

LAS Letter 249

Addressee: Esarhaddon

Date: July 2, 670 BCE

Text: (*Beginning lost*) (The prince) [. . . .] is doing well; [the king, my lord], can be happy. - What the king wrote [to me]: "Conjure Adad-šumu-uṣur! Why did he say that the crown prince and Šamaš-šumu-ukīn should not go outdoors before the 22nd day of Tašrītu? Has he (perhaps) seen some portent?" I have written (about the matter), he has been conjured in the city of Akkad. He swore by the gods of the king: "I have seen no portent; (however), until he has completed the 100 days [..." (*Break*) About the substitute king he said: "[He should go] to his destiny [on the 22nd of Tašrītu (?)]."

Comments:

Date: ... A terminus *ante ante quem*, Tašrītu 22, is furnished ...; a terminus *post quem*, Du'ūzu 14, is obtained by subtracting from this the hundred days which the substitute king had to "complete" before the two crown princes could risk going outdoors ... Since all "reigns" of substitute kings were started by eclipses, and those lasting a hundred days specifically by lunar ones, it is certain that a lunar eclipse had occurred at the latter date, Du'ūzu 14. The identification of the eclipse in question, and consequently the dating of the letter in a specific year, is made possible by the reference to the crown prince [Assurbanipal] and his brother Šamaš-šumu-ukīn ... , which shows that the event took place between the years 672 and 669 ... the only suitable eclipse visible in Mesopotamia within that span of time was that of July 2, -670. This date agrees exactly with the Babylonian date Du'ūzu 14 mentioned above ...

LAS Letter 278

Addressee: Esarhaddon

Date: July 6, 671 BCE

Text: To the king, my lord, (from) your servant Mār-Ištar: Good health to the king, my lord! May the gods Nabû and Marduk bless the king, my lord! May the great gods bestow long days, well-being and joy upon the king, my lord. As regards the lunar eclipse about which the king, my lord, wrote to me, it was observed in the cities of Akkad, Barsip, and Nippur. What we had seen in Akkad corresponded to the other (observation)s. A bronze ket[tledrum] was set up; the darkness [... (*Long break*)

I have extracted the [relevant] interpretation written on the tablet (and) s[ent] (it), together with this letter, to the king, my lord. Moreover, I shall keep the watch for the solar eclipse, as the king, my lord, wrote to me. Whether it occurs or not, I shall write to the king, my lord, whatever it be.

This lunar eclipse which took place afflicted all countries, but its whole evil heaped upon the Westland. "Westland" means the Hittite country (Syria) or, according to another interpretation, Chaldea. With the king, my lord, all is well. However, the guard should not be neglected, (and) the relevant apotropaic ritual should be performed for the king, my lord.

Comments:

Notes: 6ff. While Babylon, Borsippa and Nippur are well attested as seats of astronomical schools and sites from where astrological reports were regularly sent to Sargonid kings[481] Akkad is not; and since Akkad is here found in a position where one would actually rather expect to find Babylon, ... it might seem that the present passage supports the thesis of Landsberger, refuted above (sub *LAS* 275) according to which Akkad in Mār-Ištar's usage was just a cover name for Babylon. Such a conclusion would be premature, though; there is nothing in the passage suggesting that Akkad served as a place of *regular* astronomical observations ... the town was mentioned here simply because it was the place where Mār-Ištar *himself* had been watching the eclipse. On the reasons of Mār-Ištar's stay in Akkad see commentary to 275.

9f. "*They set up a bronze kettledrum*": referring to a ritual lamentation performed in order to appease the "angered" moon. Cf. the "Gebet an einen verfinsterten Gott" published by Ebeling, *Or* NS 17 (1948) 416ff, and the *kalû*-ritual against lunar eclipses, *BRM* 4 no. 6 (edited by Ebeling, *TuL* p. 91ff). Note also Layard, *Nineveh and Babylon* (abr. ed., 1867), p. 314f: "I gained ... some credit for wisdom and superhuman knowledge by predicting, through the aid of an almanac, a partial eclipse of the moon. It duly took place to the great dismay of my guests, who well-nigh knocked out the bottoms of all my kitchen utensils in their endeavor to frighten away the Jins who had thus laid hold of the planet. The common notion amongst ignorant Mohammedans is, that an eclipse is caused by some evil spirit catching hold of the sun or moon. On such occasions, in Eastern towns, the whole population assembles with pots, pans, and other equally rude instruments of music, and, with the aid of their lungs, make a din and turmoil which might suffice to drive away a whole army of evil spirits, even at so great a distance."

⁴⁸¹ Reports were sent from Babylon, Barsip, Cutha, Dilbat and Uruk . . . ; Pliny and Strabo mention Babylon, Borsippa, Sippar and Uruk as seats of astrological schools; *RMA* 274 refers to observatories in Babylon, Nippur, Uruk and Barsip (in this order).

LAS Letter 280

Addressee: Esarhaddon

Date: January or February 670 BCE

Text: [To the king], my [lord], (from) your servant [Mār-Ištar]: [Good health] to the king, my lord! May [the gods Nabû and Marduk] bless [the king], my lord! May [the great gods] bestow [long days], well-being and joy upon the king, my lord. [Damqî], the son of the bishop of Akka[de], who had ru[led] Assyria, Babylon(ia) [and] all the countries, [di]ed with his queen on the night o[f the . . th day as] a substitute for the king, my lord, [and for the sake of the li]fe of (the prince) Šamaš-šumu-uk[īn]. He went to his destiny for their rescue. *{Editor's note: Subsequently changed to "ransom." (See note 12 below)}*

We prepared the burial chamber. He and his queen have been decorated, treated, displayed, buried (and) wailed over. The burnt-offering has been burnt, all omens have been cancelled, (and) numerous apotropaic rituals, *bīt rimki* (and) *bīt salā' mê* ceremonies, exorcistic rites, *eršaḫunga*-chants (and) scribal recitations have been performed in perfect manner. The king, my lord, should know (this).

[I] have heard that before these ceremonies a prophetess had prophesied, saying to the son of the bishop, Damqî: "You will take over my kingship!" The prophetess had also said to him in the assembly of the country: "I have revealed the polecat (?), the . . . of my lord, I have put you into the hands (of the destiny?)." - These apotropaic rituals which were performed had a very favorable outcome; the king, my lord, can be happy.

The inhabitants of Akkad were terrified, (but) we encouraged them, (and) they calmed down. Moreover, I have heard that also the bishops (and) delegates of Akkad were terrified. Bēl and Nabû (and) all the gods have lengthened the days of the king, my lord; still, during the (validity) period of the eclipse (and) the approach of the gods he may not go to open country. - If it suits the king, my lord, a common man should, as before, be appointed to the office of the bishop, to present the regular offerings in front of the dais and, on the day of the *eššēšu*-festival and at the "Greeting of the temple" ceremony, to pour the incense for the Lady of Akkad on the censer. When [an eclipse] afflicting the land of Akkad takes place, [he] may serve as a substitute for the king, my lord, (and) stand [....]; [The ... s] of the king, my lord, would succeed, [....] the people would be calm. Let the king, my lord, appoint in his place anyone [.....] who is acceptable to the k[ing, my lord, among] his [....]s, brothers, [and ... s].

Comments:

Date: ... the 100 day period usually covered by the substitute king ritual ... was not yet over and ... at least one conjunction of the "gods" (i.e. the moon and the sun) was yet to take place before those 100 days were completed. Kanūnu 15 + 100 days gives Nisannu 25 ± 1; consequently, the letter must have been written before the preceding new moon, i.e. before the end of Addāru.

Notes: 9.... "*died on the night of* [...]": does this remark imply that the death of the substitute king and his queen was arranged through an "overdosed soporific", i.e. poisoned food or drink? This would certainly have been the most convenient way of getting rid of the two and, at the same time, of creating for the public the impression of a natural death, which doubtless lay in the interests of both the king and his aides.[487] ...

10f.... notice the clear distinction made here between the ruling king and Šamaš-šumu-ukīn as regards the purpose of the substitute king ritual; Damqî ... "went" to his fate" as *substitute* for the former, but merely *for the life* of the latter. Keeping in mind that the substitute took over all the dominions of the ruling king ... it follows that the king in question had ruled over "Assyria, Babylon and all the countries" ... and consequently can be only Esarhaddon, not Assurbanipal ... Šamaš-šumu-ukīn is mentioned here because of his position as the crown prince of Babylon, which gave him a share of royal power (cf. on *LAS* 247 and 281:5) but also entangled him, in cases like this (total eclipse of the moon), in dangers threatening the king himself. The fact that Šamaš-šumu-ukīn alone is mentioned with his father (omitting Assurbanipal) implies that the prince was resident in Babylonia while the letter was written ...

12. ... the word *pīdu* is a synonym of *pūḫu* and has therefore to be rendered "surrogate" or "ransom" rather than "rescue"...

r11-13. (3) ... "the crown prince and Šamaš-šumu-ukīn should not go outdoors before Tašrītu 22 ... until he (= the substitute king) has completed the 100 days ..."

(4) ... All these passages ... imply that it is risky for the king or his son to move outside the palace precincts during a period of time marked as unlucky by a celestial portent. ... [487] Cf. simply the euphemism *ana šimti alāku* used in referring to the execution of the substitute king in Obv. 12 and elsewhere in the present corpus.

LAS Letter 292

Addressee: Esarhaddon

Date: October 7, 671 BCE

Text: *(Beginning lost)* As [regards the su]bstitute king about whom [the king, my lord, wrote to me]: "Let him sit for a 100 days; (only) [after] he has completed the 100 days, [he should go to his fate]." [I am w]aiting [for the ...] like the king, my lord, wr[ote to me]; the king, my lord, should k[now] (this). *(The remaining lines of obverse and the beginning of reverse cannot be reconstructed with certainty; mention is made of a "blow" [obv. 6'] and of [a statue] of Esarhaddon [obv. 7'].)* ... in Bar]sip a comm[on man was ... ed (?)]; the priest of [DN], [Aḫḫīš]â, has [...]ed him, (and) they have taken everything that [...] (and) brought into the city of Barsip. Sī-li [... from TN], Nabû-zēra-ibni from Bīt-takba (?), (and) [PN] from Dūr-Šarruku: [these] altogether three [men] have been sha[ved] (and) impaled by the priest Aḫḫīšâ. [...] The statues of Sargon king [of Assyria] which were placed in the sanctuaries, [... s], (and) streets, [... on] the neck of [DN *(Rest of the letter lost except for first line of the left edge listing offerings to a deity.)*

Comments:

Discussion: ... and was consequently of no concern to Mār-Ištar.[535] By contrast, it is known with certainty that in 671 the scene of the ritual was in both cases Akkad, and it is hence a priori probable that Mār-Ištar was in both cases directly involved in the supervision of the ceremonies. The question as to which one of the two alternatives has to be chosen is settled by Obv. 2'f (stating that the substitute king had completed his 100 day reign; cf. relevant note) and Obv. 11'f (referring to a celestial observation). We know that the substitute king enthroned on account of the Du'ūzu-eclipse of 617 was due to "sit" full hundred days (cf. *LAS* 249 and relevant commentary) whereas it is very likely that the ritual following the Kanūnu-eclipse was terminated before the 100 day period was over (cf. *LAS* 280 r11 and notes on the date of the letter). The present letter would thus have been written 100 days after the occurrence of the lunar eclipse of Du'ūzu = July 2, 671, i.e. on Tašrītu 22 = October 7, 671....

Notes: 2'ff.... forced to conclude that the substitute king had actually completed his reign just before the letter was written.... translate: "Now then he has completed the 100 days, his reign is finished." ...

6'... the context ... suggests that this word somehow pertains to the final phase of the substitute king ritual, hence perhaps = "a blow (of mercy)" ... "they shall inflict blow for blow upon him, (and) he shall compensate with a life." ....[535] In the lunar eclipse of June 10, 669, only the southern quadrant of the moon (pertaining to Assyria) was touched by the earth's shadow; there was consequently no reason to have a substitute king rule in Babylonia. The solar eclipse of May 27, 669, likewise portended death for the king of *Assyria*, but not for the king of Babylonia ...

LAS Letter 298

Addressee: Assurbanipal

Date: July 30, 666 BCE

Text: To the king, [my lord], (from) your servant Akkullānu: Goo[d health] to the king, my lord! May the gods Nabû and [Marduk] bless the king, my lord! As regards the substitute statue about which the king, [my lord], wrote to his servant: "It was sitting in the city of Akkad from the 14th of Du'ūzu till the 5th of Abu", why did they act in this way? And why did they enthrone (it) in Akkad? Should they have done (it) in the city of your father where you yourself are living, it would have removed your evil! Why you? And why an evil of Akkad? Have they (perhaps) said to you on this matter: "Your father en[throned] (his substitutes) there." These (talks) are rubbish! Why did the ki[ng] not say to them like this: "[The evil] of my father [was in on]e region, mine is in [another] one; [the evil] of Assyria and Akkad [are not identical (?) . . .]: when a sign pertaining to [Assyria appears, (the ritual) should be performed here], (and) when a sign pertaining to [Akkad appears, it should be done there]." Now the king of Akkad [is well (?) . . .] I have received [. . . (*Long break*) Per[haps the king s]ays: "What is the subst[itu]te then?"

The Ser[ie]s has said (as follows) in connection with the Nisannu eclipse: "If the planet Jupiter is present in the eclipse, all is well with the king, a noble dignitary will die in his stead." Has the king paid attention (to this)? A full month had not yet passed (before) his chief judge was dead. Now the king has (already) twice performed an apotropaic ritual for him; (but) when have you actually performed one for yourself?

If I had not addressed the king today, wouldn't the king say to his servant tomorrow: "You were a servant of my father; why didn't you advise (and) instruct me?" And thus I cho[se] thes[e] words from my heart; "I shall spe[ak] in the king's presence about directing away the e[vil] of the land of Su[bartu]." I sent these words to the king, my lord (already) before, as early as on the 12th of Du'ūzu; (but) I saw the answer (only) on the 8th of Abu. Why, O king, my lord? - May the king, my lord, write to his servant (about) his health and (that) the king is happy.

Comments:

Discussion: This letter is important in that it shows that the substitute king ritual was in the Sargonid period by no means confined to the reign of Esarhaddon only (as frequently contended in the past, cf. Introduction, p. XXIII), but was also performed in the reign of Assurbanipal, though in a somewhat exceptional way – at least as far as the present case is concerned! The substitute king in question was not enthroned immediately after the eclipse, as usual, but only at the last moment, viz. when already 87 days of the 100-day eclipse period . . . had passed . . . (supposing that two of the intervening months had 30 days). Why so? The answer is given by *LAS* 299, which doubtless is the "previous letter" Akkullānu in Rev. 27' claims to have sent to the king on the 12th of Du'ūzu, i.e. *two days before* the substitute began his 20-day reign in Akkad. In that letter Akkullānu draws the king's attention to the fact that nothing had been done for months to counteract the evil portents of a recent eclipse of the moon ... and warns that unpleasant consequences may follow from such negligence ... As an appropriate counter measure he suggests that one should, among things, perform an exorcistic ritual called "giving a man's substitute to Ereškigal", and adds that the king should stay in his palace while the ritual was being performed in "another region" ... There can't be any doubt that it was exactly because of this letter that the substitute king was hurriedly enthroned in the city of Akkad, and it would seem that the king himself had given the pertinent order, to judge from the manner in which he informs his servant on the fait accompli (present letter ...). No doubt the king had believed to have followed the instructions of his adviser exactly but, unfortunately as Akkullānu's indignant reaction shows, he had utterly misunderstood these. He had evidently taken it for granted that "giving a man's substitute to Ereškigal" meant the substitute king ritual which had been repeatedly performed under his father, and had consequently taken Akkullānu's "other region" to mean Babylonia and specifically the city of Akkad, which had served as the scene of the ritual every time it had not been performed in Nineveh. From the "scientific" point of view, the performance of the ritual in this case was an obvious mistake. First, no substitute king at all would have been needed, since Jupiter had been "present" in the eclipse ..., as Akkullānu had already pointed out in his earlier letter (*LAS* 299:6'f). Second, there was absolutely no reason to enthrone a substitute in Akkad, since the eclipse concerned Assyria, not Babylonia ... By having a substitute "sit" in Akkad the king had only been able to assure the safety of the king of Akkad ..., i.e. Šamaš-šumu-ukīn, but had done nothing whatsoever for his own welfare ... Little wonder that Akkullānu was so upset. It is hard to believe that any of the king's other scientific advisers, whom Akkullānu seems to accuse for {what} happened, could have acted so ignorantly; it is more likely – as already pointed out above – that the king had acted on his own, perhaps believing that on the ground of his careful education he was able to handle the seemingly straight-forward case properly, and the present letter would thus provide an illustration of how profound the king's schooling actually was (cf. commentaries on *LAS* 34 and 331). A further detail in the letter bearing on the early history of Assurbanipal is also worth noticing: in spite of the unjust split of the empire between Assurbanipal and Šamaš-šumu-ukīn (cf.

LAS 129 with notes), the two brothers were in 666 obviously still in perfectly brotherly terms, for it is unconceivable that Assurbanipal could otherwise have so quickly enthroned a substitute in Akkad, which lay within the confines of the kingdom of his brother – even granting that the action was to the advantage of the latter.

Notes: r10'f. . . . "If the Moon makes an eclipse and Jupiter is present in that eclipse, the king will be well; a noted dignitary will die in his stead."

LAS Letter 299

Addressee: Assurbanipal

Date: July 5, 666 BCE

Text: (*Beginning lost; after obv. 2'* [the Moon] was eclip[sed, *there follow two fragmentary lines where only the words* oxen *and* horses *are intelligible*) . . . But attention should be paid to ransoming (?) the king's [. . .]! "When it (*or* he) emerges during it, the king will be well." I have now brought out this matter (and) spoken to the king; have we now . . . ed our case [li]ttle (?) or much? And what is the harm? [The king should indeed pay] attention to this matter, [Why], up to now, [the king] has not given [. . .]? (*Small break*) A reed [. . .] should be constructed, and (the ritual) "Giving a person's substitute to the Queen of the Netherworld" should be performed. You should stay in your palace, let them perform (the rituals) in another place. Why is nothing done month after mo[nth]? [It is] a fault! Something [will cert]ainly [ensue] from it! [. . . . . .] Assyr[ia . . . (*Remainder lost*)

Comments:

Notes: 3'f. "Oxen and horses": unclear; perhaps some casualty portended by the eclipse."

Chapter 9

The Babylonian Substitute King Ritual and Christ's Redemptive Death

THIS IS THE UPDATED English translation of a paper titled "Babylonialainen sijaiskuningasrituaali ja Kristuksen sovituskuolema," which was presented at the meeting of the Finnish Oriental Society on February 2, 1985.

The Babylonian Substitute King Ritual and Christ's Redemptive Death

(by Simo Parpola)

In his speech "On Kingship" addressed to Emperor Trajan, Dio Chrysostomus gives the following account of the Sakaia ritual performed by the Persians:

> They take a prisoner condemned to death, seat him upon the throne of the king, robe him in royal garments and let him issue orders, drink and revel, yes, during those days he is even allowed to amuse himself with the king's concubines, and nobody prevents him from doing what he wants. Then, however, he is dragged out, whipped, and hanged.[1]

Theologians and cultural anthropologists have already long been interested in this strange spectacle, which is occasionally referred to elsewhere too in classical literature and Babylonian and Persian historical tradition, and which also seems, among other things, to have given rise to the theme "caliph for a day" in the story of Abu-l-Ḥasan the Wag or

---

1. See Chapter 7, *Catalogue of sources and references to the ritual*, No. 16, p. 75.

The Sleeper Awakened in *One Thousand and One Nights*. The reality hidden behind all these different tales and anecdotes has, however, started to become clear only during the past few decades. An important turning point was the discovery of letters in the royal archives of Nineveh showing that the rite described by Dio had already been practiced at the Assyrian royal court in the seventh century BC. A fragmentary text containing detailed directions for the performance of the ritual was later discovered in the same archives. The German Hittitologist Hans Martin Kümmel has recently published more similar directions, this time from the Hittite capital Hattusha and dating to the 14th century BC. These texts are written in Hittite, but numerous details indicate that they too are based on Babylonian originals. Thus it is evident that the rite in question originated in Babylonia, from where it already early spread to other parts of the ancient Near East.

In Babylonian texts, the object of the rite, the individual robed as king is called *šar pūḫi*, "substitute king". This confirms the hypothesis already presented on the basis of the classical tradition, that we are dealing with a substitution ritual, in which a person robed as king temporarily took the place of the real king. But how often, in what connection, and, above all, *why* was such a substitution ritual practiced in the first place? Answers to these questions have been obtained only recently from the cuneiform texts. The storytellers and narrators of anecdotes mostly do not seem to have had any idea of the real nature of the rite they described.

Dio Chrysostomus thinks the purpose of the rite was to remind Persian kings of mortality:

> What do you think this festival stands for? And why do the Persians celebrate it? Isn't the idea as follows: the power and title of the king is often grabbed by stupid and vicious men, who for a while indulge in revelries and soon find an infamous death. Therefore, it is also natural that the ignorant fool rejoices and congratulates himself when freed from his chains, but the one who knows laments bitterly, resists from being taken along, and would much rather remain in chains as before. You, too, fool, don't try to be a king before you have got reason![2]

According to James Frazer's famous attempt at interpretation, the substitute king ritual was part of the New Year's festival of Babylon, after which the king, who had originally been elected for one year only, should have died in accordance with an age-old custom. When the critical days

2. Ibid, No. 16, p. 75.

approached, the king would have abdicated his crown and let a substitute die in his stead. Frazer clearly owes this interpretation to Athenaeus of Naucratic (c. AD 230), who claims that the Sakaia-festival was celebrated yearly in Babylon as a five-day carnival. Although this claim has no basis whatever, the notion of the substitute king ritual as some kind of a cruel farce only has evidently been as popular in the past as it is today. In the *Arabian Nights*, the actions of Abu-l-Ḥasan as caliph are presented as so amusing that the real caliph, who observes them through a cleft in the curtain, is nearly choked by laughter. This "farce interpretation" of the ritual was developed to the extreme by Mika Waltari. Book Six of his *Sinuhe the Egyptian* is a fierce burlesque inspired by Frazer and *One Thousand and One Nights*, where wine flows and King Burraburiash laughingly accepts humiliations, while the mob storms to ram slave Captah on the throne of Babylon "on the Day of the False King."

The reality, however, was different.

The substitute king ritual is not referred to as a farce in any cuneiform text. It was not part of the New Year's festival nor of any other public festival, and, more importantly, it was not performed regularly on a specific day or days of the year. The cause of the ritual was evil signs portending the death of the king, especially eclipses of the sun or the moon. The ritual manual found in Nineveh unambiguously states: "The person given instead of the king shall die, but the evil omens will not touch the king himself; he is safe and this country will thrive." The pertinent evil omens are then defined as follows: "(This will happen) because of the evil portent of bad and inauspicious signals and signs of heaven and earth, because of the eclipse of the moon, the eclipse of the sun, or the eclipse of Jupiter, Venus and other planets in such-and-such month and on such-and-such day."[3]

In the royal correspondence of Nineveh there are references to altogether eight performances of the substitute king ritual, and in all of them the ritual was performed because of an eclipse of the moon or the sun. However, not all eclipses automatically required the performance of the ritual. Although according to Mesopotamian astrology an eclipse of the moon or the sun *always* foreboded the death of a significant king, Babylonian or Assyrian kings came into question only if a precisely defined part of the lunar disc was eclipse. An analysis of the eclipses that occurred during the Ninevite correspondence demostrates that the ritual was indeed resorted

---

3. Ibid, No. 3, p. 69.

THE SUBSTITUTE KING RITUAL AND CHRIST'S REDEMPTIVE DEATH

to only if this condition was fulfilled, in other words, only when the eclipse specifically signified the death of an Assyrian or Babylonian king.

Evil omens clearly are the cause of the ritual also in some classical sources. Plutarch relates the following anecdote in his *Life of Alexander*:

> As he was upon his way to Babylon, Nearchus came to tell him he had met with some Chaldean diviners, who had warned him against Alexander's going thither. Alexander, however, took no thought of it, and went on, and when he came near the walls of the place, he saw a great many crows fighting with one another, some of whom fell down just by him ... Beside this, he was disturbed by many other prodigies ... And one day after he had undressed himself to be anointed, and was playing at ball, just as they were bringing his clothes again, the young men who played with him perceived a man clad in the king's robes with a diadem upon his head, sitting silently upon his throne. They asked who he was, to which he gave no answer for a good while, till at last, coming to himself, he told them his name was Dionysios, that he was from Messenia, that for some crime of which he was accused he was brought thither from the seaside, and had been kept long in prison, that Serapis appeared to him, had freed him from his chains, conducted him to that place, and commanded him to put on the king's robe and diadem, and to sit where they found him, and to say nothing. Alexander, when he heard this, by the direction of his soothsayers, put the fellow to death.[4]

The same event is described in two other lives of Alexander as well, in the *Anabasis* of Arrian and the *Universal History* of Diodorus Siculus. The part of evil omens in the incident emerges from both narratives at least indirectly. Arrian writes:

> A certain man of obscure condition (some say that he was even one of the men kept under guard without being held in chains), seeing the throne and the couches empty, walked through lines of eunuchs, ascended the throne, and sat upon it. According to a Persian law, they did not make him rise from the throne, but rent their garments and beat their breasts and faces as if on account of a great wail. When Alexander was informed of this, he ordered the man who had sat upon his throne to be put to the torture, with the view of discovering whether he had done this according to a plan concerted by a conspiracy. But the man confessed nothing, except that it came into his mind at the same time to act thus. Even more

---

4. Ibid, No. 15, p. 73.

for this reason the diviners explained that this occurrence boded no good to him.⁵

Diodorus, on the other hand, presents the incident as follows:

> As the king was having himself anointed and the royal garment and the diadem were lying on a couch beside the throne, a native prisoner freed himself from his chains and, unnoticed by the guards, made his way through the doors into the hall without anybody trying to stop him. He went to the throne, dressed in royal robes, put on the diadem, sat upon the throne and remained quiet. When the incident was noticed, the king, though frightened by it, went to the throne and, concealing his fright, calmly asked the man who he was and for what purpose he had done it. As he answered that he was aware of no reason whatever, the king consulted the soothsayers about the omen and then, by their direction, put the man to death so as to make the unlucky portents turn against him. Himself, he dressed again in his robes and sacrificed to the protective gods, but felt restless. He remembered the prophecy of the Chaldeans and castigated the philosophers who had persuaded him to enter Babylon, admiring the skill of the Chaldeans and their vision.⁶

None of the three historians mention which omen or omens made the Chaldeans conclude that Alexander had better stay away from Babylon and in the end resort to the subtitute king ritual in order to save him. It is, however, likely that the reason was the complete solar eclipse of May, 324 BC. Alexander died in June of the next year.

In addition to eclipses, some other portents as well were interpreted to predict the king's death, for example, comets. We shall return to them later on.

The descriptions of the substitute king ritual performed for Alexander just cited reveal three central features of this rite, which also become apparent from Assyrian and Hittite sources:

1. The decision to perform the ritual was made and practically implemented by court scholars, the highest authorities of the realm in the field of divination, magic and religion. The king issued the order to execute the substitute king, but did not necessarily otherwise interfere in the course of events.

5. Ibid, No. 15a, p. 74.
6. Ibid, No. 15b, p. 74.

THE SUBSTITUTE KING RITUAL AND CHRIST'S REDEMPTIVE DEATH

2. The substitute king was a prisoner or a simple person, whose life was not much valued.
3. The royal bodyguards and the court knew well the significance of the ritual. In contrast, the substitute king himself was not necessarily aware of it. His primary role was to sit silently on the throne dressed in the king's robes, carrying the royal insignia.

Recently published Assyrian documents reveal that notwithstanding his passive role, the substitute king was not kept hidden in the royal palace, but he could travel from one city to another surrounded by an escort of hundreds of people (mostly bodyguards). Such gorgeous travelling may well have given rise to the *One Thousand and One Nights* story of "The False Caliph" making nocturnal boat trips. It also explains the misunderstanding of some classical authors like Dio Chrysostomus that the substitute king would have enjoyed full royal power during his "reign". In reality, the substitute had no power whatsoever, and the bodyguards escorting him were there only to make sure that the thought of turning his kingship into a more permanent one wouldn't come into his head. According to Babylonian chronicles, once in the distant past (about 1860 BC) a gardener selected as substitute king had managed to rise to kingship after the real king had died while devouring hot porridge. It is remarkable that the Byzantine historiographer Agathias, who lived in the sixth century CE, still found this incident worth mentioning.

The "reign" of the substitute king varied in length. Its theoretical maximum length was a hundred days, during which time period the death of the king portended by the eclipses would come true according to the astrological doctrines. The Ninevite royal correspondence refers to two cases where the substitute king indeed "reigned" for a hundred days. Most often, however, the ritual was terminated considerably earlier, after a few weeks or only a few days. This shows that its length had in principle no great significance. From the viewpoint of the king, the sooner the ritual ended the better, for he had during its performance to keep hidden in his palace and absolutely away from publicity. Extending the ritual seems to have been required only by practical reasons like new inauspicious omens observed after its beginning. Such a case is known for instance from the following letter:

> Concerning the substitute king about whom the king, my lord, wrote to me: "How many days should he sit (on the throne)?"—we

waited for a solar eclipse, but the eclipse did not take place. Now, if the gods are seen together on the 15th day, he may go to his fate on the 16th. Alternatively, if it is agreeable to the king, my lord, let him complete the 100 days. (*LAS* 135)

From our viewpoint, a much more essential aspect in the ritual than its length or other practical details is its ideological basis. In order to understand it better, we have to consider more closely the substitute king's coronation rites, which are described in three letters found in Nineveh. All these letters are addressed to the king, although in the extract cited first he is modestly entitled "farmer":

To the "farmer", my lord: your servant Nabû-zeru-lešir. Good health to my lord! May Nabû and Marduk bless my lord for many years! I wrote down whatever signs there were, be they celestial, terrestrial or of malformed births, and had them recited in front of Šamaš (the celestial judge), one after the other ... The substitute king of the land of Akkad took the signs on himself. (*LAS* 30)

The next report pertains to a ritual performed eight years later, but the situation is the same:

Concerning the signs about which my lord wrote to me, after we had enthroned him, we had him hear them in front of Šamaš. Furthermore, yesterday I had him hear them again, and cut them out and bound them in his hem. Now I shall again do as my lord wrote to me. (*LAS* 26)

The third extract relates to a ritual performed half a year after the preceding one:

The substitute king, who on the 14th sat on the throne in Nineveh and spent the night of the 15th in the palace o[f the kin]g, and on account of whom the eclipse took place, entered the city of Akkad safely on the night of the 20th and sat upon the throne. I made him recite the scholarly litanies before Šamaš; he took all the celestial and terrestrial portents on himself, and ruled all the countries ... With the king, my lord, all is well; the king, my lord, will attain his desire, and the deeds and prayers of the king, my lord, are acceptable to the gods ... Nevertheless, the king, my lord, should be on his guard and under strong protection. (*LAS* 279)

In the ritual described here, a Babylonian nobleman kept as hostage in the Ninevite court had exceptionally been selected as the substitute king, with the explicit aim to frighten Babylonian seditionists who were harbouring separatistic dreams. His fate excited extraordinary attention and commotion in Babylonia, as shown by the following letter reporting on his death:

> Damqi, the son of the prelate of Akkad, who had ruled Assyria, Babylon and all the countries, died with his queen on the night of the [... th] day as a substitute for the king, my lord, and for the sake of the life of Šamaš-šumu-ukin. He went to his fate for their redemption. We prepared the burial chamber. He and his queen were decorated, treated, displayed, buried and wailed over. The burnt-offering was made, all portents were cancelled, and numerous apotropaic rituals, *Bīt rimki* and *Bīt salā' mê* ceremonies, exorcistic rites, penitential psalms and scholarly recitations were performed to perfection.
>
> The king, my lord, should know that I have heard that before these ceremonies a prophetess prophesied, saying to the son of the prelate, Damqi: "You will take over the kingship." The same prophetess also told him in the assembly of the country: "I have revealed the polecat, the ... of my lord, and placed him in your hands." These apotropaic rituals which were performed succeeded well indeed; the king, my lord, can be glad. The inhabitants of Akkad became terrified, (but) we gave them heart and they calmed down. Moreover, I have heard that the prelates and delegates of Babylonia got terrified, too. Bel and Nabû and all the gods have lengthened the days of the king, my lord; still, during the (validity) period of the eclipse he should not go into open country. (*LAS* 352)

Many details in these letters would deserve comment, but we must here concentrate on the essentials.

First of all, it is worth paying attention to the way in which the king was addressed during the ritual. I have already drawn attention in passing to the appellation "farmer" occurring in some letters. This way of addressing the king is found only in the correspondence pertaining to substitute king ritual, and it has hence been already long ago suggested that it would reflect a sort of "change of roles" built into the ritual. According to this theory, in order to evade the fate, the king would during the ritual have assumed the role of the person chosen as the substitute, who in his turn would have entered the role of the king. It has to be noted, however, that the person chosen as the substitute normally was *not* a farmer but a prisoner sentenced to death. Even more remarkable is that the address "farmer" was by no means used consistently but the king could even during the ritual be quite normally addressed as "the king, my lord". Furthermore, it has to be noted that the person chosen as the substitute king was in no phase called "king", but always unambiguously the king's *substitute,* once even by his own name. Therefore the idea of a complete change of roles has to be discarded. The appellation "farmer", which was one of the religious titles of the Mesopotamian kings as incarnations of the saviour god, Ninurta, probably was merely used as an euphemism meant to emphasize the king's humbleness during the ritual.

The substitute king ritual was thus by no means only a sort of masquerade naïvely purporting to deceive fate, but the king remained king and the substitute a mere substitute from the beginning to the end. This conclusion is supported by the following anecdote related by Herodotus:

> But when night came, again the same vision stood over Xerxes as he slept, and said, "Son of Darius, it seems thou hast openly before all the Persians renounced the expedition, making light of my words, as though thou hadst not heard them spoken. Know therefore and be well assured, that unless thou go forth to the war, this thing shall happen unto thee thou art grown mighty and puissant in a short space, so likewise shalt thou within a little time be brought low indeed."
>
> Then Xerxes, greatly frightened at the vision which he had seen, sprang from his couch, and sent a messenger to call Artabanus, who came at the summons, when Xerxes spoke to him in these words: "Artabanus, at the moment I acted foolishly, when I gave thee ill words in return for thy good advice. However it was not long ere I repented, and was convinced that thy counsel was such as I ought to follow. But I may not now act in this way, greatly as I desire to do so. For ever since I repented and changed my mind a dream has haunted me, which disapproves my intentions, and has now just gone from me with threats. Now if this dream is sent to me from God, and if it is indeed his will that our troops should march against Greece, thou too wilt have the same dream come to thee and receive the same commands as myself. And this will be most sure to happen, I think, if thou *puttest on the dress which I am wont to wear, and then, after taking thy seat upon my throne,* liest down to sleep on my bed."
>
> Such were the words of Xerxes. Artabanus would not at first yield to the command of the king; for he deemed himself unworthy to sit upon the royal throne. At the last, however, he was forced to give way, and did as Xerxes bade him; but first he spake thus to the king: "Now thou sayest that . . . a dream has haunted thee,

sent by some god or other, which will not suffer thee to lay aside the expedition. [If] God has indeed some part therein, let it even appear to me as it has to thee, and lay on me the same injunctions. But it ought not to appear to me anymore if I put on thy clothes than if I wear my own, nor if I go to sleep in thy bed than if I do so in mine—supposing, I mean, that it is about to appear at all. For this thing, be it what it may, that visits thee in thy sleep, *surely is not so far gone in folly as to see me, and because I am dressed in thy clothes, straightway to mistake me for thee."*

Thus spake Artabanus; and when he had so said, thinking to show Xerxes that his words were naught, he did according to his orders. Having put on the garments which Xerxes was wont to wear and taken his seat upon the royal throne, he lay down to sleep upon the king's own bed. As he slept, there appeared to him the very same dream which had been seen by Xerxes; it came and stood over Artabanus, and said: "Thou art the man, then, who, feigning to be tender of Xerxes, seekest to dissuade him from leading his armies against the Greeks! But thou shalt not escape scathless, either now or in time to come, because thou hast sought to prevent that which is fated to happen. As for Xerxes, it has been plainly told to himself what will befall him, if he refuses to perform my bidding." In such words the vision threatened him, and then endeavoured to burn out his eyes with red-hot irons . . . [7]

This anecdote, of course, does not pertain to a substitute king ritual in its proper sense, but it contains all the essential elements of it. As Herodotos specifically mentions having heard the story from the Persians themselves, it can be taken for sure that the ritual was regularly practiced in the court of Xerxes. And the passage also makes it perfectly clear that the person substituting the king kept his identity during the entire course of the ritual.

How then was it thinkable that the death of the substitute king could rescue the king?

The answer, and in actual fact the key to the whole ritual, is hidden in the Mesopotamian understanding of omens. Omens were not just strange natural phenomena, as we are wont to think nowadays, but signs sent by gods invisibly ruling the world, *signals*, which could be interpreted with the help of handbooks given by the gods themselves. This is evident already from the Akkadian word for "omen, sign", *ittu*, which frequently occurs in the meanings "notice", "signal" and even "light signal". The nature of omens as signals is clearly stated in the so-called *Babylonian Diviner's Almanach*:

7. Ibid, No. 14, p. 72.

> Heaven and earth together give us signs; they are given separately but they are not in contradiction with each other, for heaven and earth are interconnected. A sign that is bad in the heaven, is bad on the earth; A sign that is bad on the earth, is bad in the heaven.

Omens were directed in the first place to kings ruling over the visible world as proxies of God. Their purpose was to guide the king to rule his country justly. If the king exercised his rule justly and piously, he and his country thrived. If he ruled unjustly, he was sinful and brought divine wrath upon himself, and, in the end, if nothing helped, received the punishment that he deserved. The destiny that he himself was shaping with his deeds was announced to him through omens.

The moral content given to omens and the manner in which they were understood clearly emerges from the following letter to the Assyrian king:

> The king, my lord, wrote to me: "The king will be slighted with his dignitaries—what losses will ensue?" (The omen the king has in mind) is the earthquake. It has quaked, and that is bad. They should perform the ritual against the earthquake, your gods will then make the evil pass by. "Ea has done, Ea has undone." He who caused the earthquake also created the apotropaic ritual against it. Was there no earthquake in the times of the king's fathers and grandfathers, and did I not see earthquakes when I was small? (With this sign) the god has wanted to open the king's ears: "He should pray to God, perform the apotropaic ritual and be on his guard." (*LAS* 35)

It is important to note especially the end of the letter, which indicates that omens were understood as *personal warnings* to the king, the purpose of which was to shake the king religiously, make him understand his state, repent and pray to god. The god-destined fate announced by the sign was irrevocable in itself, but it could be atoned and made to bypass the king by performing an absolving ritual created by god himself. In the case of an earthquake, the misfortune destined for the king was relatively slight, and his sin correspondingly little. In that case it was customary to cut the king's nails and body hair, enclose them in a bottle and take the bottle to an enemy country, whereupon the "unclean spirit" closed in the bottle sufficed to direct the misfortune to its finder. Eclipses told of much graver sins, which could be atoned only with death.

From this basis, we can understand why it was necessary for the coronation of the substitute king to include a recitation ceremony where the

THE SUBSTITUTE KING RITUAL AND CHRIST'S REDEMPTIVE DEATH

substitute was forced to repeat orally the evil omens pertaining to the ritual in the presence of the sungod Šamaš, the celestial judge. Because the omens had been directed to the king *personally*, merely abdicating the crown and enthroning a substitute king under no circumstances sufficed for annulling the fate destined for him. It was essentially important to make the substitute receive the omens, and with them, the king's burden of sin, before the celestial judge. In case the substitute could not or would not repeat the omens, the same purpose was reached by tying a list of omens written on papyrus to his body.

This ceremony demonstrates that the designation "substitute *king*" actually is, in a sense, misleading. The substitute had to be king in order for the prophecies of canonical omen collections to come true, but otherwise the aspect of kingship was secondary, as far as he was concerned. His proper role was to function as scapegoat, *surrogate sufferer*, who took upon himself the sins of the king and atoned them with his blood. This idea underlies the letter cited above, where it is said of the dead substitute king: "He went to his fate for their redemption."

In this juncture, it is good to recall how the substitute, according to Greek historians, sat on the throne: silently. As surrogate sufferer he symbolized a *sacrificial lamb*, like which he had to go to his destiny silently. That the scapegoat-sacrificial-lamb symbolism indeed underlied the substitute king ritual appears with all clarity from a Babylonian ritual titled *pūhi amēli ana Ereškigal* or "Giving a substitute of the man to Ereshkigal", which in its content forms an almost perfect parallel to the substitute king rite. In this ritual, a virgin kid is sacrificed to infernal gods as a substitute for a fatally ill patient, with the following words:

> "The kid is the substitute of the man, he thus gives the kid in his stead. The head of the kid he gives for the man's head, the neck of the kid he gives for the man's neck, the breast of the kid he gives for the man's breast", and so on.

However, we need not take refuge to Ancient Mesopotamia to find an even closer parallel: *the suffering and death of Christ*. The similarities between the substitute king ritual and the passion of Jesus are so obvious and remarkable that they probably need not be analyzed here in detail. Suffice it to refer to Jesus' silence before Caiphas and Pilate, his coronation with the crown of thorns, his title "King of the Jews" fixed on the cross, the solar eclipse on the day of crucifixion, and the famous words of John: "Behold, the Lamb of God, who takes away the sins of the world!"

In the same breath it has to be made clear that it is not possible to take the passion story simply as another case of the substitute king ritual. Externally the course of the events is the same: a prisoner sentenced to death is crowned king and put to death as sacrificial lamb. The big difference is that the role of the sacrificial lamb was *forced* on the substitute king by his executors, whereas Jesus espoused this role out of his own volition. It cannot be excluded, however, that he was in fact crowned and executed as a substitute king in order to get rid of a dangerous rebel leader and to make the evil of the predicted solar eclipse fall upon him, as in the case of the Babylonian prelate's son, Damqi, cited above (*LAS* 352).

In any case, I would claim that the links between the substitute king ritual and Christ's passion are not accidental. The ancient Near East, including Palestine, was a large commercial and cultural area where goods and ideas moved freely irrespective of linguistic or other boundaries. The center of this cultural area was Mesopotamia, and ever since the annexation of the northern kingdom of Israel by the Assyrians in the eighth century BC and especially after the Babylonian exile, the Jews were in constant contact with Mesopotamia and absorbed innumerable stimuli from there in the fields of culture, science and religion.

It is clear that the substitute king ritual and the "surrogate sufferer" ideology underlying it must have been much better known all over the ancient Near East than one would be prone to think. Even though it was not a popular celebration regularly repeated every year, it is certain that at least in the Assyrian and Babylonian royal courts, a substitute king was on average needed every second year, sometimes even twice a year. We have already seen that the ritual was, besides Assyria and Babylonia, also practiced among the Hittites and in the courts of Xerxes and Alexander the Great, and it continued to be practiced in the Roman empire as well, and even much later. In his *Life of Nero*, Suetonius relates:

> It chanced that a comet had begun to appear on several successive nights, a thing which is commonly believed to portend the death of great rulers. Worried by this, and learning from the astrologer Balbillus that kings usually averted such omens by the death of some distinguished man, thus turning them from themselves upon the heads of the nobles, he resolved on the death of all the eminent men of the State.[8]

---

8. Ibid, No. 18, p. 76.

THE SUBSTITUTE KING RITUAL AND CHRIST'S REDEMPTIVE DEATH

A similar story is also included in the life of the emperor Claudius (AD 41–54); the ritual probably entered Rome with Chaldean astrologers. In Persia it was certainly practiced as late as AD 1591, as appears from the following extract from John Malcolm's classical *History of Persia*:

> While engaged in preventing the inroads of the Usbegs, he (Abbas the Great) was suddenly called from all considerations of foreign or domestic policy, by a prediction of his astrologers; who, from the aspect of the heavenly bodies, had discovered that a most serious danger impended over the sovereign of Persia. Abbas was not exempt from the superstition of the age in which he lived, and did not hesitate to adopt the strange expedient by which his counsellors proposed to avert the dreaded omen. He abdicated the throne; and a person of the name of Yusoofee, whom Persian authors take care to tell us was an unbeliever (probably a Christian), was crowned; and for three days, if we are to believe these historians, he enjoyed not only the name and state, but the power of the king. The cruel farce ended as was to be expected. Yusoofee was put to death; the decree of the stars was fulfilled by this sacrifice; and Abbas, who reascended his throne in a most propitious hour, was promised by his astrologers a long and glorious reign.[9]

The ritual was thus performed for thousands of years over a wide geographical area, from Rome to Persia. There is no reason to doubt that is was known in Roman Palestine as well. And although it in principle was an internal affair of the royal court, many facts indicate that it was well known even among the ordinary people. I would here again draw attention to the Assyrian letter *LAS* 352 just mentioned, where a female prophet prophesies to the substitute king in the "assembly of the country". This letter was written in 671 BC, about a hundred years before Second Isaiah wrote his famous verses about the "suffering servant of the Lord" (Isaiah 53:3–7):

> He was despised, he shrank from the sight of men, tormented and humbled by suffering; we despised him, we held him of no account, a thing from which men turn away their eyes. Yet on himself he bore our sufferings, our torments he endured . . . He was pierced for our transgressions, tortured for our iniquities . . . We had all strayed like sheep, each of us had gone his own way; but the Lord laid upon him the guilt of us all. He was afflicted, he submitted to be struck down and did not open his mouth, he was led like a sheep to the slaughter, like an ewe that is dumb before the shearers.

9. Ibid, No. 19, p. 76.

The entire public career of Jesus demonstrates that he considered himself the god-sent saviour whose appearance was predicted in Daniel 9:24–27 to "bring sin to an end and usher in everlasting righteousness". On the other hand, his understanding of his mission differed radically from the popular notion of Messiah at his time and was clearly based on Isaiah 53. Even if the Second Isaiah, who lived in Babylon, knew nothing about the substitute king ritual, which is extremely unlikely, the fact remains that the idea presented in his prophecy of a "suffering servant" shouldering the sins of others like a sacrificial lamb was the central idea of the substitute king ritual as well. Thus, paradoxically, the analysis of a Mesopotamian ritual confirms the traditional understanding of one of the most central dogmas of Christianity.

Chapter 10

Jesus the Substitute King

THE NINEVEH RECORDS DISCUSSED in the last three chapters show without a doubt that under Assarbanipal, the last Assyrian monarch, the Assyrians killed substitutes *in Babylonia* and maintained the priestly bureaucracy and observation systems needed to sustain that process. But did the Neo-Babylonians continue to seat substitutes for their kings? We have no archaeological records to prove it, but plenty of Scripture (much of which we have reviewed) testifies that they did. In addition, the Babylonians worshipped the same gods as the Assyrians, and entrenched beliefs and bureaucracies would not have been easily abandoned.

But here is the most convincing proof that the Neo-Babylonians sacrificed substitute kings: As Parpola proves, the Assyrians used substitute kings before the Neo-Babylonians, and the Persians used substitutes after the Neo-Babylonians. Surely the Neo-Babylonians also practiced substitution.

Now we are ready to move from the sixth century BCE to the first century CE.

As we shall see, the gospel of Mark goes into detail to portray that Jesus, the second Son of Man, died like a substitute king, just as Ezekiel had. But did Jesus himself grasp the nature of this role? If he understood the inner meanings of Scripture's Suffering Servant texts, then he also knew what lay ahead for him. Jesus was a master of Hebrew Scripture. He devoted time to schooling his disciples in it and also in debating the Scriptures with critics.

As we traced in an earlier chapter, there was a pipeline of scriptural interpretation that reached over the centuries between the Exile and the opening century of our era. That pipeline extended from Isaiah 52 through the Dead Sea Scrolls. Was Jesus himself aware of the references to how Ezekiel had met his end centuries before? We think so. The Suffering Servant and the Jesus stories met and were combined in Mark's gospel. And we should not assume that Mark was the first to reach this conclusion. Jesus himself must have made the connection. He deeply understood Scripture, and would have been the very first to grasp the similarities between his own mission and the mission (and fate) of the first Son of Man.

Consider New Testament Scriptures.[1] Jesus "was teaching his disciples ... 'the Son of Man is to be betrayed into human hands, and they will kill him, and three days after being killed, he will rise again'" (Mark 9:31). A direct hit upon Ezekiel's substitution! This next passage from Matthew also refers to the Hebrew Scriptures. After the priests arrested him, Jesus told his resisting followers to put away their swords, since Scripture had forecast that he would be seized in that manner. Then Jesus added, "All this had taken place, so that the Scriptures of the prophets may be fulfilled" (Matt 26:54, 56). Which prophets? Start with Ezekiel and the concealed references to the Jerusalem uprising, and proceed to Isaiah 53 with its account of the Suffering Servant. And if Jesus understood Isaiah 53, he almost certainly knew the substitute king secret.[2]

Jesus says it best in Luke's gospel. After his death, on the road to Emmaus Jesus appeared to two disciples: "Beginning with Moses and all the prophets, he interpreted to them all the things *about himself* in all the Scriptures" (Luke 24:27, emphasis added). At greater length, he told them, "'everything written about me in the law of Moses, the prophets, and the psalms must be fulfilled.' Then he opened their minds to understand the Scriptures, and he said to them, 'Thus it is written, that the Messiah is to suffer and to rise from the dead on the third day, and that repentance and forgiveness of sins is to be proclaimed in his name to all nations, beginning from Jerusalem'" (Luke 24:45–47). The disciples reflected, "Were not our hearts burning within us ... while he was opening the Scriptures to us?" (Luke 24:32).

Reading Luke, then, we propose that Jesus (or his disciples) decided that substitute kingship well described the Son of Man's death and resurrection, and that they passed these secrets along to those who were to write the synoptic gospels. What followed is that *the gospel writers framed their narratives to portray Jesus as a substitute king!* The synoptic writers drew heavily

---

1. Appendix 3 lists all the New Testament's Son-of-Man verses.

2. Limbaugh, *Emmaus Code*, 337–43. This book offers an appendix with six score messianic prophecies in Hebrew Scriptures.

on the substitute king motif, particularly for their passion accounts. Mark provided the bulk of the items, but Q, Luke, and Matthew also contributed. These authors braided together in the New Testament many strands of the substitute king tradition.

After the failed Jerusalem uprising, in addition to Ezekiel, Babylonian authorities sacrificed as substitutes at least Asaiah, Jehoiachin, and Daniel. Quite likely there also were other Jewish martyrs whose deaths might have inspired different Scriptures. The substitute king motif within the gospels has more aspects than one can now identify, but here is a start.

Jesus King of the Jews

These are kingly parallels. The devil took Jesus to "a very high mountain" to tempt him with the world's kingdoms (Matt 4:8). Ezekiel received a similar offer—to rule Babylon's splendid empire. And as icing, by using "a very high mountain," Matthew implied a reference to the Tower of Babel—a ziggurat that was termed "The Mountain" in a drama performed during Babylon's New Year's Festival.[3]

In another parallel, Jesus asked how it benefited a man to gain the world and forfeit his life (Mark 8:36). Ezekiel paid with his life after gaining one of the world's most magnificent kingdoms. Before the high priest, Jesus quoted Daniel 7: "You will see the Son of Man seated at the right hand of the Power" (Mark 14:62). The next morning, when taken before the Roman authorities, Pilate asked Jesus directly, "Are you the King of the Jews?" And Jesus made the nonanswer, "You say so." (Mark 15:2–3). (Centuries earlier, Ezekiel, too, had at first refused to assume kingship.) Pilate next asked the crowd, "Do you want me to release to you the King of the Jews?" Hearing no good answer, Pilate asked the crowd what it wished him to do with "the King of the Jews." When they answered "crucify him," Pilate surrendered Jesus to the Roman soldiers, who repeated the charge "King of the Jews" as they beat him (Mark 15:9–15).

The Babylonians put royal robes on the first Son of Man, and gave him a crown and a scepter. Soldiers attired Jesus in a purple cloak and crown of thorns (Mark 15:17), to which Matthew's account added a mock scepter (Matt 27:29). *LAS* 134 to Assyrian king Esarhaddon said, "As regards the substitute king of Akkad [Babylon], order should be given to enthrone him. As regards the clothes of the king, my lord, and the garments of the statue

---

3. Pallis, *Akitu Festival*, 221–22.

of the substitute king, as regards the necklace of gold, the scepter and the throne *break* . . . "

Ezekiel's crime was that he was king of Babylon and, as a result, had scores of soldiers watching him. Parpola's *Excursus*, reference 6a, reports on tablets detailing wine rations to an Assyrian substitute's court. The issues of wine per person served 320, one-third of whom were bodyguards.

When Jesus was before the whole cohort of soldiers, they "began saluting him, 'Hail, King of the Jews!'" (Mark 15:18). When they crucified him, "the charge against him read, 'The King of the Jews'" (Mark 15:25). Mark works that memorable title into his crucifixion narrative five times (Matthew has three and Luke two). Reading Mark 15, one could wonder why he so often used that phrase. Also, the author never again reverted to "Son of Man." In Mark's gospel, Son of Man had given way to the new substitute, King of the Jews, though that term was always put in the mouths of others.

There are additional substitute king signals. Jesus asked, "The wedding guests cannot mourn as long as the bridegroom is with them, can they?" (Matt 9:15). Matthew's use of "mourn" emphasized the short time between the marriage and death. Ezekiel became a bridegroom when authorities compelled him to marry a substitute queen, and days later they put him to death.

The substitute king motif continued. Ezekiel and Jesus both bore the title Son of Man. Ninety-three repetitions of the title were credited to the prophet in the book of Ezekiel, with just ten fewer to Jesus in the New Testament books. These are amazing totals. Further, authorities anointed Ezekiel as a king, and centuries later Peter declared Jesus to be the Christ, the anointed one (Mark 8:29). Ezekiel would have led a coronation parade through Babylon and, disabled by torture, might well have been mounted on an ass.[4] The parallel is that Jesus rode a colt during his regal Palm Sunday entrance into Jerusalem (Mark 11:7, 9). Moreover, Luke's version of the procession inserted "the King" into a line from Psalms. According to him the crowd shouted, "Blessed is *the King* who comes in the name of the LORD!" (Luke 19:38, emphasis added; compare Ps 118:26). Very likely, to present Jesus as a potential king, the gospel writers were evoking the coronation traditions of Judah (see 1 Kgs 1:32–40 and 2 Kgs 11).[5] If anything, however, these served as further camouflage for the deeper substitute king secret.

---

4. See also Zech 9:9. Ecclesiastes wrote of servants on horses (Eccl 10:7). The preacher may have had in mind the Suffering Servant, since previous verses mentioned "sun" and "folly seated on high."

5. For Judean coronation traditions, see von Rad, "Royal Ritual in Judah."

Another parallel is that as Babylon's temporary king, Ezekiel had to host sumptuous banquets, while Jesus hosted the Last Supper (Mark 14:17–26).[6] At other times, Jesus was accused of being a glutton and a drunkard (Matt 11:19). Moreover, the first Son of Man—Ezekiel—sat upon a throne, and it was said of Jesus that when the second "'Son of Man comes in his glory . . . he will sit on the throne of his glory'" (Matt 25:31).

Jesus Redeems Rebels

Previous chapters touched upon Ezekiel's disgust with Cyrus and the mess that Judah's rebellions against Babylon had made. Despite the prophet's innocence, the Babylonians apparently thought him a rebel, for Isaiah 53 mentions rebellion frequently. The Suffering Servant was wounded for rebellions, stricken for rebellions, and numbered with rebels (Isa 53:5, 8, 12). The synoptic gospel writers took pains to picture Jesus in the same way. Jesus directed his followers to buy swords so that he himself might be "'counted among the lawless [rebels]'" (Luke 22:36–37). Also, authorities used weapons to seize Jesus as though taking "a bandit" (Mark 14:48).[7] And of course a supporter of Jesus struck the high priest's slave (Mark 14:47). Jesus freed the rebel Barabbas (Mark 15:15), just as Ezekiel freed the rebel captives. Likewise, Jesus's mission included proclaiming release to captives (Luke 4:18), and Ezekiel freed imprisoned Judeans. Finally, at the end, Jesus hung between two outlaws (Mark 15:27).

As a substitute king, Ezekiel had to endure a lengthy cursing ceremony. In parallel, Jesus faced numerous charges, and was as silent in the face of them (Mark 15:4–5) as Ezekiel had been (Isa 53:7). Jesus questioned whether his disciples were able to drink the cup that he was to drink (Mark 10:38), and later asked God to "'remove this cup from me'" (Mark 14:36). According to a Nineveh letter, substitute kings were "treated" with wine before their enthronement ceremonies. In addition, the ancients may have dispatched their substitute kings with poison (though the Babylonians probably beheaded Ezekiel).[8] Both Jesus (Mark 15:15) and Ezekiel (Isa 53:5) endured flogging and, like Ezekiel, Jesus was handed to foreigners to die (Mark 10:33). On the cross, the chief priests mocked Jesus: "'He saved others; he cannot save himself'" (Mark 15:31), while Ezekiel

---

6. Parpola II, XXV.
7. Funk and Hoover, *Five Gospels*, used "rebels."
8. Parpola I, 21; Parpola II, XXVI, 271.

gave himself up to save others. When Jesus died, tombs were opened (Matt 27:52); in parallel, the Suffering Servant agreed to die so that prisons could be opened. The substitute king took sins to the nether world, and Jesus had authority to forgive sins (Mark 2:10).

And this is especially interesting: Disciples asked Jesus why the scribes said that Elijah's coming would precede that of the messiah (Mark 9:11). The scribes seemed to know that a solar eclipse preceded the Suffering Servant's coming. The two words "Elijah" and "sun" in Greek have almost identical spellings, and the book of Malachi has the two words close together. In the Septuagint, Mal 4:2 has "sun [helios] of righteousness," and verse 4:5 says, "I will send you the prophet Elijah [Helias] before the great and terrible day of the LORD comes." Closely related to this, a midday eclipse found Jesus on the cross (Mark 15:33), and an eclipse at that very same hour led to Ezekiel's death.

In Assyria (and surely in Babylon) officials burned a dead substitute's regal symbols of office, but not his clothes.[9] Probably Ezekiel's guards split his royal wardrobe among themselves, and they well may have thrown dice for it. Psalm 22:18 said, "They divide my clothes among themselves, and for my clothing they cast lots." As for Jesus, soldiers gambled for his garments (Mark 15:24).

Substitute kings had royal burials. "We prepared the burial chamber," an official reported to the king of Assyria, and went on to describe the ceremony, which included spices and embalming.[10] Thus, Ezekiel was buried with royalty. Isaiah 53:9 described it this way: "They made his grave with the wicked and with a rich man in his death." According to Mark's gospel, Joseph of Arimathea donated his new tomb for burial (Mark 15:43). Joseph, though probably well off, was a follower of Jesus, and therefore certainly not wicked. Matthew's gospel solved half the problem by calling Joseph rich (Matt 27:57).

Other burial practices in the gospels seem to have substitute traditions as their source. Three women brought embalming spices to treat Jesus (Mark 16:1). The parallel was that Ezekiel's body was treated with spices. Jesus's body was laid in a new tomb (Matt 27:60), while Mesopotamian substitutes went to a royal "burial chamber."[11] In the gospel of Matthew, Jesus spoke of "the coming of the Son of Man." Then he continued, "Wherever

---

9. Lambert, "Substitute King Ritual," 110.
10. Parpola I, 229.
11. Ibid.

the corpse is, there the vultures will gather" (Matt 24:27–28). But what can the Son of Man have to do with vultures around a body? A lot, if Jesus referred to the funeral of the original Son of Man. For burial of his mother, one Babylonian king assembled "people from far-off provinces, he summoned even kings, princes and governors."[12] When kings and governors flocked to bury Ezekiel, they came like vultures to a corpse. Moreover, in Greek Scripture, the words "son," "and," "man," and "vulture" occurred together only twice—in Ezek 17:2–3 and in Matt 24:28 (the vulture passage). Both contained these very words, making a Word Link. The Ezekiel passage even included the prophet's title, "son of man."[13] The author of Matthew was making a parallel for knowing readers between Jesus and Ezekiel the substitute, whose body had drawn the dignitary-vultures. The symbol for burial chamber was E KI.MAH. The E added "house" to the word for tomb or grave. The term frequently occurred with royalty, such as the burials for King Assurbanipal and for the wife of King Esarhaddon.[14]

Finally, Ezekiel's death voided curses upon king and people alike. An Assyrian reported to King Essarhaddon in 670 that Damqî died "as a substitute for the king, my lord, and for the sake of the life of the prince Šamaš-šumu-ukīn. He went to his destiny *for their ransom*"[15] (emphasis added). Compare this to the words of Jesus in Mark 10:45: "'For the Son of Man came not to be served but to serve, *and to give his life a ransom for many*'" (emphasis also added).

Reevaluation Needed

Had the Jesus Seminar scholars heard of these things when they were evaluating New Testament texts? No, they had not. We first drew the New Testament implications from the events outlined above more than a decade after Funk's *The Five Gospels* reached publication.[16] That book briefly highlighted Jesus's use of Son of Man (*Five Gospels* used "Adam"). The book said, "The confusion in how this phrase is to be understood owes to the fact that the Christian community tended to understand the phrase messianically

---

12. Gadd, "Nabonidus Inscriptions," 53.

13. In translating the Hebrew Scriptures, the NRSV substituted "mortal" for "son of man," so where appropriate we have used the RSV.

14. Reiner, *Assyrian Dictionary*, 8:370–71.

15. Gadd, "Nabonidus Inscriptions," 53.

16. Kavanagh, *Exilic Code*, 125–33.

or apocalyptically. The original senses derived from the Hebrew Bible were lost or suppressed."[17] The renowned Jesus Seminar scholars of course evaluated and scored every quote and phrase in each gospel. In the end, they judged that 82 percent of the words ascribed to Jesus in the gospels were not actually spoken by him.[18] However, at the time, scholars did not know that Ezekiel, the original Son of Man, was the subject of Isaiah 53, let alone that the prophet died as a substitute king.

Eighty-two percent, carefully considered by such a company, is difficult to argue with, especially when combined with the differences in wording between the synoptic gospels, and the fact that our earliest manuscript fragments date a century or more after Jesus's death. On top of these considerations comes another even more recent discovery. According to John Shelby Spong, Mark (and later the gospels of Matthew and Luke) was developed within the synagogue, and both chronology and content were tailored to fit the sequence of Scripture used within the Jewish liturgical year.[19] This is a finding of first importance. Spong writes that during synagogue services, "Followers of Jesus would stand and recall their memories of Jesus as the readings for that Sabbath elicited such memories . . . this clearly was the context in which stories of Jesus were passed on during the oral period."[20] And Spong continues, "Sabbath by Sabbath, year by year, in synagogue after synagogue the stories of Jesus were related to the Jewish Scriptures read in worship, and this was the process in which the gospels were formed, orally at first, but later written down . . ."[21]

Spong's findings, plus the scholarly offerings of the Jesus Seminar, plus manuscript dating and differences, bring into question the extent to which the New Testament can tell us who Jesus was or what he did. To this perplexing stew please add my own discoveries. These include a Son-of-Man connection between Ezekiel and Jesus, which no other scholar now imagines. The prophet, the first Son of Man, forced Nebuchadnezzar to free the captive Jews who filled Babylon's prisons and holding pens. Ezekiel's death was thus redemptive, and when Jesus assumed the Son-of-Man title, he claimed to be like Ezekiel, with redemptive death followed by rising

---

17. Funk and Hoover, *Five Gospels*, 77.

18. Ibid, 5.

19. Spong, *Reclaiming the Bible*, 222–25. See also Spong's *Biblical Literalism: A Gentile Heresy*.

20. Ibid, 225.

21. Ibid.

from the dead ahead of him. As Mark's gospel states, "He began to teach them that the Son of Man must undergo great suffering, and be rejected by the elders, the chief priests, and the scribes, and be killed, and after three days rise again" (Mark 8:31). That is, Jesus taught his disciples that his life experience was to be very like Ezekiel's, the Son of Man who first died as a substitute king. Mark, Matthew, and Luke drew upon the Son-of-Man secret to frame their passion narratives. This became a hinge of Scripture, upon which the synoptic gospels turned.

Quoting the Jesus Seminar scholars again, "The original senses [of the term "Son of Man"] derived from the Hebrew Bible were lost or suppressed." Lost they may have been, but found they now are. In view of the fresh information in this book, we ask that scholars reevaluate why Jesus called himself the Son of Man.

Appendix 1

Athbash Letter Exchanges

AFTER SELECTING THE LETTERS of the true word on line 1, go to another line and substitute column-by-column to form the true word's athbash equivalent.

Appendix 2

Eclipses Enthroning Substitute Kings During the Babylonian Exile

(41 OF 81 ECLIPSES, 0 to 10 probability of causing substitution)

Date 6th C. BCE	Type (Lunar, Solar)	Prob SubK 0–10
8/4/98	L	7
7/9/97	S	9
5/9/94	S	8
3/22/91	L	10
5/28/85	S	7
10/27/84	L	10
10/16/83	L	8
3/16/81	S	10
2/19/80	L	8
8/14/80	L	10
2/8/79	L	5
1/14/78	S	8
12/7/77	L	10
4/1/73	L	10
9/14/72	L	10
1/5/69	S	6
7/15/69	L	9

ECLIPSES ENTHRONING SUBSTITUTE KINGS

Date 6th C. BCE	Type (Lunar, Solar)	Prob SubK 0–10
1/7/68	L	8
11/7/66	L	9
5/2/65	L	10
10/27/65	L	8
4/7/64	S	8
9/5/63	L	8
3/2/62	L	10
2/19/61	L	6
8/14/61	L	10
4/23/56	L	6
10/6/55	L	10
3/18/54	S	8
9/26/54	L	9
8/31/53	S	9
2/9/52	L	8
7/15/50	L	7
9/15/45	L	9
3/27/44	S	7
7/31/42	S	10
1/10/41	L	10
7/5/41	L	8
12/29/41	L	9
6/24/40	L	9
6/13/39	L	7

Appendix 3

Influence upon Son-of-Man Verses in New Testament

(I for Isaiah 53 influence, D for Daniel 7 influence, U for undetermined)

MARK ALONE AND WITH PARALLELS

I	Mark 2:10 forgive sins	Matt 9:6, Luke 5:24
I	Mark 2:28 lord of Sabbath	Matt 12:8, Luke 6:5
I	Mark 8:31 suffer, rejected, killed, rise	Luke 9:22
D	Mark 8:38 ashamed of man	Matt 16:27, 28, Luke 9:26
I	Mark 9:9 quiet until raised	Matt 17:9
I	Mark 9:12 suffer many things	
I	Mark 9:31 delivered to men, kill, rise	Matt 17:22, Luke 9:44
I	Mark 10:33 chief priests, mock, scourge, kill, rise	Matt 20:18, Luke 18:31, 24:7
I	Mark 10:45 to serve and ransom	
D	Mark 13:26 power, angels, elect	Matt 10:23
I	Mark 14:21 twice woe to betrayer	Matt 26:24 twice, Luke 22:22
I	Mark 14:41 betrayed to sinners	
D	Mark 14:62 priest will see Power	Luke 22:69

INFLUENCE UPON SON-OF-MAN VERSES IN NEW TESTAMENT

MATTHEW ALONE AND WITH LUKE PARALLELS

I	Matt 8:20 lay head, foxes, birds	Luke 9:58
I	Matt 11:19 glutton, drunkard	Luke 7:34
U	Matt 12:32 sin against Holy Ghost	Luke 12:10
D	Matt 12:40 sign of Jonah	Luke 11:30
D	Matt 13:37 sowing good seed	
D	Matt 13:41 sends angels, burns evildoers	
D	Matt 16:13 Christ, son of God	
I	Matt 17:12 suffer at hands	Luke 17:25
I	Matt 18:11 omitted verse, came to save	Luke 19:10
D	Matt 19:28 and 25:31 glorious throne	
I	Matt 20:28 serve, life as ransom	
D	Matt 24:27 comes like lightning	Luke 17:24
D	Matt 24:30 sign in heaven (twice)	
D	Matt 24:37 coming like Noah	Luke 17:26
D	Matt 24:44 unexpected coming	Luke 12:40
I	Matt 26:2 to be crucified	
I	Matt 26:45 betrayed to sinners	

LUKE AND ACTS ONLY

I	Luke 6:22 blessed when reviled
D	Luke 11:30 sign of Jonah
D	Luke 12:8 acknowledged before angels
D	Luke 17:22 not see days
D	Luke 17:30 fire, brimstone
D	Luke 18:8 comes will he find faith
D	Luke 21:27 power, glory coming
D	Luke 21:36 last day stand before
I	Luke 22:48 Judas kiss
D	Acts 7:56 sees Steven stoned (quotes Dan 7:16)

APPENDIX 3

JOHN AND REST OF NEW TESTAMENT

D	John 1:51 angels descending
D	John 3:13 descended from heaven
I	John 3:14 Moses lifted serpent
D	John 5:27 authority for judgment
U	John 6:27 food, eternal life
U	John 6:53 eat flesh, blood
D	John 6:62 disciples see ascending
U	John 8:28 speaks with authority
U	John 12:23 hour come for glorified
U	John 12:34 say lifted up
U	John 12:34 who is this
U	John 13:31 now glorified
U	Heb 2:6 care for him (references Ps 102:25)
D	Rev 14:14 seated on cloud (cites Dan 7:13)

List of Abbreviations used in Chapters 7–9

ABL   R. F. Harper, *Assyrian and Babylonian Letters* (London and Chicago 1892–1914)
ACh   Ch. Virolleaud, *L'astrologie chaldéenne* (Paris 1907–12)
AfO   *Archiv für Orientforschung*
AnSt   *Anatolian Studies*
AOAT   *Alter Orient und Altes Testament*
BRM   *Babylonian Records in the Library of J. Pierpont Morgan*
CAD   *The Assyrian Dictionary of the Oriental Institute of the University of Chicago*
CT   *Cuneiform Texts from Babylonian Tablets in the British Museum*
CTN   *Cuneiform Texts from Nimrud*
IRSA   E. Sollberger et J. R. Kupper, *Inscriptions royales sumeriennes et akkadiennes*. Paris: Les Éditions du Cerf, 1971.
LAS   S. Parpola, *Letters from Assyrian Scholars to the Kings Esarhaddon and Assurbanipal* I–II (AOAT 5/1–2, Neukirchen-Vluyn 1970, 1983)
ND   field numbers of tablets excavated at Nimrud
Or NS   *Orientalia*, Nova Series
RA   *Revue d'assyriologie et d'archéologie orientale*
RMA   R. C. Thompson, *The Reports of the Magicians and Astrologers of Nineveh and Babylon* I–II (London 1900)
StOr   *Studia Orientalia*
TCS   *Texts from Cuneiform Sources*
TuL   E. Ebeling, *Tod und Leben nach den Vorstellungen der Babylonier* (Berlin and Leipzig 1931)

LIST OF ABBREVIATIONS USED IN CHAPTERS 7–9

ZA   *Zeitschrift für Assyriologie und Vorderasiatische Archäologie*
Col.   Column
MB   Middle Babylonian
OB   Old Babylonian
Rev., r.   Reverse
Spl.   Supplement

Glossary

Anagrams—Anagrams used some or all the letters within Hebrew text words to spell hidden names. Letter sequence was ignored and athbash variations of names were regularly employed. For example, "whoring," as frequently used by Ezekiel, contains an anagram of "Huldah." See Kavanagh, *The Exilic Code*, 21–27.

Athbash—Athbash generates twenty-one other ways to spell any Hebrew word. It divides the Hebrew alphabet in half to form facing rows of letters. Eleven letters run right-to-left; the other eleven run left-to-right. Next, tractor-tread rotation changes the interfaces, allowing the parallel rows of letters (with one adjustment) to generate twenty-one new ways to spell a name. Athbash is discussed more fully in Kavanagh, *Secrets of the Jewish Exile*, 198–205.

Chi-squares—A frequently used statistical calculation that this book employs to test how well groups of anagrams or coded spellings in a passage (usually a chapter) match their frequency in the remainder of Scripture. The answer is given in probability of occurrence. See Statistically Significant.

Coded Spelling—Encoded spellings use one—and only one—letter from consecutive text words to spell a name. A five-letter name would borrow a letter from five Hebrew text words in a row. Letters chosen could fall in any sequence. Kavanagh, *The Exilic Code*, 6–13, discusses this further.

Deuteronomistic History—DH includes Deuteronomy 5–28, Joshua, Judges, First Samuel, Second Samuel, First Kings, and Second Kings.

Diaspora—Refers to Jews living outside of Israel during and after the sixth century BCE.

Exile—Refers to the 597–539 BCE period, when the Babylonians exiled the members of the upper levels of Judean society.

Group of Coded Spellings—Group is defined as a statistically significant concentration of the same coded spelling within a single chapter. Spellings within a group range from one to close to one hundred. Counting groups is a handy way to compare the coding strength of different names within a chapter or book. The completed calibration of Jewish personal names against Scripture produces 1.7 million groups.

GLOSSARY

Jacob, Second Isaiah—Second Isaiah is thought to have written Isaiah 40–55. His true name was Jacob (see Kavanagh, *The Exilic Code*, 62–84) and his father's name was probably Isaac. Jacob worked closely with Huldah and defended her in the book of Proverbs.

Micaiah—Micaiah the scribe was the son of Gemariah and the grandson of Shaphan. Micaiah served in the court of King Jehoiakim and was presumably exiled to Babylon in 597 BCE. Encoded spellings of Micaiah's name in the DH outnumber all others, making him the best candidate for leader of the Dtr group.

Statistically Significant—Statistical significance addresses the probability of occurrence, with above .001 being the point of exclusion. Significance grows with rarity. Groups of encodings or anagrams are generally the things so measured.

Word Links—A Word Link connects two passages that have in their texts the same unique batch of words. That particular batch will appear nowhere else in Scripture except in those two passages. (See Kavanagh, *The Exilic Code*, 62–84.)

Bibliography

Albertz, Rainer. *Israel in Exile: The History and Literature of the Sixth Century BCE.* Atlanta, Society of Biblical Literature, 2003.
Black, Matthew. *The Book of Enoch or I Enoch: A New English Edition with Commentary and Textual Notes.* Studia in Veteris Testamenti Pseudepigrapha 7. Leiden: Brill, 1985.
Böhl, Franz Marius Theodor de Liagre. *Opera minora: Studies en bijdragen op Assyriologisch en Oudtestamentisch terrein.* Groningen-Djakarta, 1953.
Boling, Robert G. "Book of Judges." In *IBD* 3:1007–17.
Borg, Marcus J. *Evolution of the Word: The New Testament in the Order the Books Were Written.* Harper Collins, 2012.
Bottéro, Jean. "Le substitut royal et son sort en Mésopotamie ancienne." *Akkadica* 9 (1978) 2–24.
Clifford, Richard J. "Second Isaiah." In *ABD* 3:490–501.
Collins, John J. "Essenes." In *ABD* 2:624.
Dhorme, Édouard. "Rituel funeraire assyrien." *RA* 38 (1941) 57–66.
Driver, G. R. "Isaiah 52:13—53:12: the Servant of the Lord." *In Memoriam Paul Kahle,* edited by Georg Fohrer, 90–105. BZAW 103. Berlin: Topelmann, 1968.
Ebeling, Erich. "Beiträge zur Kenntnis der Beschwörungsserie Namburbi." *RA* 48 (1954) 1–15, 76–85, 130–141, 178–191; 49 (1955) 32–41, 137–148, 178–192; 50 (1956) 22–33, 86–94.
———. "Ein Gebet an einem 'verfinsterten Gott' aus neuassyrischer Zeit." *Or* NS 17 (1948) 416–422.
Funk, Robert W., et al. *The Five Gospels.* San Francisco: HarperSanFrancisco, 1997.
Gadd, C. J. "The Harran Inscriptions of Nabonidus." *AnSt* 8 (1958) 35–92.
———. "Three Roman Parallels." *AfO* 18 (1957–58) 318.
Gurney, O. R. "The Sultantepe Tablets; the Eponym Lists." *AnSt* 3 (1953) 15–21.
Jacobsen, Thorkild. "Early Political Development in Mesopotamia." *ZA* 52 (1957) 91–140.
Josephus. *The Works of Josephus.* Peabody: Hendrickson, 1987.
Kavanagh, Preston. *The Exilic Code: Ciphers, Word Links, and Dating in Exilic and Post-Exilic Biblical Literature.* Eugene, OR: Pickwick Publications, 2009.
———. *Huldah: The Prophet Who Wrote Hebrew Scripture.* Eugene, OR: Pickwick Publications, 2012.

BIBLIOGRAPHY

———. *Secrets of the Jewish Exile*. Tarantium, PA: Word Association, 2005.
———. *The Shaphan Group: The Fifteen Authors Who Shaped the Hebrew Bible*. Eugene, OR: Pickwick Publications, 2011.
Klouda, Sheri L. "Isaiah's Use of Psalm 97 in Isaiah 60 and 62." Presentation to the 2005 Convention of the Society for Biblical Literature.
Kümmel, H. M. *Ersatzrituale für den hethitischen König*. Studien zu den Boğazköy-Texten 3. Wiesbaden: Harrassowitz, 1967.
Labat, René. "Le sort des substituts royaux en Assyrie au temps des Sargonides." *RA* 40 (1946) 123–142.
Lambert, W. G. "A Part of the Ritual for the Substitute King." *AfO* 18 (1957–58) 109–12.
———. "The Ritual for the Substitute King—a new Fragment." *AfO* 19 (1959–60) 119.
Landsberger, Benno. *Brief des Bischofs von Esagila an König Asarhaddon*. Amsterdam: Noord-Hollandsche Uitgevers Maatschappij, 1965.
Lane, E. W. *The Arabian Nights*. London 1889.
Layard, Austen H. *Nineveh and Its Remains*. London 1849.
Liid, Dale. "Tower of Eder." In *ABD* 2:284.
Limbaugh, David. *The Emmaus Code*, Washington, D.C., Regnary Publishing, 2015.
Lott, Jeffrey. "Migdol." In *ABD* 4:822.
Lowery, K. E. "Jehizkiah." In *ABD* 3:658.
Malcolm, John. *History of Persia*, Vol. I. London 1829.
Mallowan, Max. "Cyrus the Great (558–529 B.C.)." *Iran* 10 (1972) 1–17.
Nickelsburg, G. W. E. "Son of Man." In *ABD* 6:137–56.
Pallis, Svend Aage. *The Babylonian Akitu Festival*. Historisk-filogiske meddelelser 12.1. Copenhagen: Bianco Lunos, 1926.
Parpola, Simo. *Letters from Assyrian Scholars to the Kings Esarhaddon and Assurbanipal: Texts*. AOAT 5. Kevalaer: Butzon & Berker, 1970. (Parpola I)
———. *Letters from Assyrian Scholars to the Kings Esarhaddon and Assurbanipal: Commentary and Appendices*. AOAT 5. Kevalaer: Butzon & Berker, 1983. (Parpola II)
———. *Letters from Assyrian Scholars to the Kings Esarhaddon and Assurbanipal, Part II A: Introduction and Appendixes*. PhD diss., University of Helsinki, 1971.
Paul, Shalom. "Literary and Ideological Echoes of Jeremiah in Deutero-Isaiah." *Proceedings of the Fifth World Congress of Jewish Studies* 1, 102–120. Jerusalem, World Union of Jewish Studies, 1969.
Porton, Gary G. "Sadducees." In *ABD* 5:892–5.
Pritchard, James B., ed. *Ancient Near Eastern Texts Relating to the Old Testament*. 3rd ed. Princeton: Princeton University Press, 1969.
Reiner, Erica, ed. *The Assyrian Dictionary*. Chicago: Oriental Institute of the University of Chicago, 1971.
Roberts, Bleddyn J. "Athbash." In *IDB* 1:306–7.
Saldarini, Anthony J. "Pharisees." In *ABD* 5:289–303.
Schott, A. and J. Schaumberger. "Vier Briefe Mâr-Ištars an Asarhaddon über Himmelserscheinungen der Jahre-670/668." *ZA* 44 (1941–42).
Spong, John Shelby. *Reclaiming the Bible for a Non-Religious World*. New York: Harper Collins Publishers, 2011.
Tadmor, Hayim. "The Inscriptions of Nabunaid." In *Studies in Honor of Benno Landsberger*, 351–64. Assyriological Studies 16. Chicago: University of Chicago Press, 1965.

Thomas, D. Winton. "Miscellanea: A Consideration of Isaiah LIII in the Light of Recent Textual and Philological Study." *ETL* 44 (1968) 79–86.
Vermes, Geza. *The Complete Dead Sea Scrolls in English*. New York: Penguin, 1998.
von Rad, G. "The Royal Ritual in Judah." In *Theological Dictionary of the Old Testament*. Grand Rapids, Eerdmans, 1995.
von Soden, Wolfram. "Beiträge zum Verständnis der assyrischen Briefe über die Ersatzkönigriten," in K. Schubert, J. Botterweck, and J. Knobloch (eds.). *Vorderasiatische Studien: Festschrift für Prof. Dr. Viktor Christian gewidmet von Kollegen und Schülern zum 70. Geburtstag* (Wien, 1956), 100–107.
———. *Herrscher im Alten Orient*. Berlin–Göttingen–Heidelberg: Springer Verlag, 1954.
———. "Texte zum assyrischen Begräbnisritual." *ZA* 43 (1936) 253–254.
Walton, John H. "The Imagery of the Substitute King Ritual in Isaiah's Fourth Servant Song." *JBL* 122 (2003) 734–43.

Index of Subjects and Modern Authors

Albertz, Rainer, 20
Alexander the Great, 12, 116
anagrams, 2, 9–12, 16–25, 34–37, 39, 43–44, 47, 55, 137–38
Apocrypha, 4
Asaiah, 16–19, 24–25, 28, 36, 39, 47, 121
Asherah, 23
Assurbanipal, 59, 62, 69, 78, 95, 98, 100–103, 125
Assyria, 3, 5–6, 17, 37–41, 58–60, 62–63, 65–67, 71, 78–80, 82, 86, 89, 97–102, 105–9, 111, 114, 116–17, 119, 121–22, 124–25
Assyrian kings, 3, 59–103
athbash, 2, 7–9, 12, 19–20, 24–25, 33, 129, 137
Babylon, 3, 5–7, 9–12, 14, 16, 18, 20–40, 42, 44–46, 51–52, 55–56, 59, 62, 65–66, 69, 71, 73, 75–76, 79–80, 82–83, 89, 91, 93, 95–98, 100, 102, 104–9, 111, 115–16, 118–19, 121–26, 130, 137–38

Baruch, 3, 9, 16–19, 21–25, 36
Black, Matthew, 48
Böhl, F. M. de Liagre, 60
Boling, Robert G., 24
Borg, Marcus, 51–52
Bottéro, Jean, 60

Churchill, Winston, 1
Clifford, Richard, 32
Collins, John, 48
Cyrus, 2–3, 9–12, 17–26, 35–36, 39, 44, 56, 123

Daniel, 3–4, 13, 17–19, 21, 24–25, 28, 32–37, 39, 41, 43–47, 54, 121
Day of Atonement, 39
Dead Sea Scrolls, 4, 48, 120
Dhorme, Édouard, 60
Driver, G. R., 38
Dtr, 2, 13, 138

Ebeling, Erich, 94, 96, 135
eclipses, 3, 5, 27–28, 47, 61–63, 65, 69–71, 79, 81–82, 95–96, 106, 108–9, 114, 130–31
Egypt, 3, 16–17, 21–26, 30, 32, 37, 44
elders, 3, 9, 18, 21–24, 52, 57, 127
encoded spellings, 2, 19–21, 33, 137–38
Esarhaddon, 5, 125
eternal life, 4, 6, 40–49, 52, 134
Evil-Marduk, 34
Excursus, 5, 27, 59–77, 122
Ezekiel
    as Son of Man, 3–4, 6, 29–30, 32, 37, 41–45, 47–48, 51–52, 55–56, 59, 122–23, 125–27
    as substitute king, 3–4, 6, 26–41, 47, 51–52, 59, 123, 126–27

INDEX OF SUBJECTS AND MODERN AUTHORS

Ezekiel (*continued*)
    as Suffering Servant, 3, 6, 26–43, 45, 48, 51–52, 59, 120, 123–24
    redeems rebels, 123
Ezra, 3, 16–19, 21–23, 39

Frazer, James, 105–6
Funk, Robert W., 6, 53, 56, 58, 123, 125–26

Gadd, C. J., 76, 125
Grayson, S. K., 68
Gurney, O. R., 70

Huldah, 2–3, 9, 16–17, 21–25, 36, 39, 43–44, 137–38

Jacob, 3, 7–8, 16–19, 21–23, 25, 36, 43–44, 138
Jacobsen, Thorkild, 74
Jehizkiah, 34–35
Jehoiachin, 2–3, 9, 10–11, 14–19, 21, 22–23, 25, 27, 29, 33–36, 38–40, 44, 47, 121
Jehoiakim, 138
Jeremiah, 7, 9, 18, 21–22, 32, 36, 44
Jericho, 24
Jerusalem, 9–12, 16–17, 19–26, 28, 30–31, 33–37, 39, 44, 56–57, 120–22
Jesus
    Ezekiel connection, 51, 126
    King of the Jews, 6, 115, 121–22
    substitute king motif, 119, 121–27
    use of Scripture, 119–21
    use of Son of Man, 119–21
Jesus Seminar, 4, 53, 55, 57–58, 125–27
Jozadak, 3, 16–19

King of the Jews, 6, 115, 121
Kinnier Wilson, J. W., 66, 69–71
Klouda, Sheri L., 13
Kümmel, H. M., 60, 69, 74, 105
Kupper, J. R., 68, 135

Labat, René, 60, 69
Lambert, W. G., 69
Landsberger, Benno, 60, 96

Lane, E. W., 77
Layard, Austen H., 77, 84, 96
Liid, Dale, 32

Malcolm, John, 76, 117
Mallowan, Max, 11
Melchizedek, 9
Micaiah, 13, 21, 138

Nebuchadnezzar, 3, 12, 19, 22–24, 26–31, 33–38, 40, 45, 56–57, 126
Nickelsburg, G. W. E., 46, 55
North, C., 31

Pallis, Svend Aage, 121
Paul, Shalom, 29, 37
Persians, 6, 23, 38, 47, 55, 75, 104–5, 112–13, 119
Porton, Gary G., 48
Pritchard, James B., 38
probabilities, 2, 13

Queen Mother, 2, 9, 21–22, 36, 43–44

Rassam, Hormuzd, 81
Reiner, Erica, 125
Roberts, Bleddyn J., 7

Sakaia ritual, 104
Saldarini, Anthony, 48
Salonen, E., 69
scapegoat, 36–37, 65, 69, 115
Schott, A., 60
Second Isaiah, 2, 4, 8, 10–12, 15–17, 21–23, 25, 32, 36, 43–44, 117–18, 138
Seleucids, 55
Sollberger, E., 68, 135
Son of Man, 1, 2, 4, 20, 28–29, 36–37, 42, 47–57, 127, 132
    Ezekiel, 3–4, 6, 29–30, 32, 37, 41–45, 47–48, 51–52, 55–56, 59, 122–23, 125–27
    inter-testament, 26–50
    Daniel, 7, 46–49, 51, 53, 55
    Jesus, 1, 6, 25, 27, 41, 49, 51–53, 55, 57–58, 119–27

INDEX OF SUBJECTS AND MODERN AUTHORS

Spong, John Shelby, 126
substitute king, 3–6, 20, 26–29, 31–36, 38–41, 43, 45–52, 55, 58–74, 76–77, 79–83, 85–90, 92–95, 98–102, 105–6, 108–24, 126–27, 130–31
    Assyrian substitute king ritual, 5, 59–103
    Babylonian substitute king ritual, 6, 104–18
    gospels framed, 119–25
Suffering Servant, 1–4, 6, 13–15, 28–29, 31–35, 37, 40, 42–43, 45, 48–49, 51–55, 59, 117–20, 122–24

Thomas, D. Winton, 38
Tyre, 16

Vermes, Geza, 48
von Rad, G., 122
von Soden, Wolfram, 60, 68, 87

Waltari, Mike, 106
Walton, John H., 31
Wiseman, D. J., 69–70
Word Link(s), 2, 3, 12–16, 19–20, 25, 28–29, 32, 55–56, 125, 138

Index of Ancient Documents

Old Testament

Genesis

14	9, 12
14:16–23	19
14:18	9
14:20–21	9
24	21
24:3	21
24:4	21
24:67	21
25	16
25:21–26	16
25:26	16

Leviticus

16	39
16:16	39
16:21	36
16:23	36

Numbers

22:4	18
22:7	22

Deuteronomy

5–28	2, 13, 137
17	43, 49
17:18–20	43
17:20	42
25:1	17

Joshua 20, 24, 137

5:13–15	24
10:4	18
10:6	18

1 Samuel 137

7:12–13	19
12:19	17

2 Samuel 137

1:19–22	25
1:27	25
21:2	18

INDEX OF ANCIENT DOCUMENTS

1 Kings	137
1:32–40	122
8:32	17

2 Kings	14–15, 35, 137
10:5	22
11	122
12:11	19
25:7	35
25:27	11
25:27–30	2, 28
25:28	29

2 Chronicles	
6:23	17
28:12	34
28:15	34
34:10	19
34:17	19

Nehemiah	
3:31	19
6:16	19

Job	4
16	49
25:4–6	43
32:9	23

Psalms	20, 111, 120
8	44, 49
8:3–6	45
22:18	124
23	33–34
55	11
55:21–22	11
86:17	17
89	43, 49
89:47–48	43
102:25	134
110	9
110:1–4	10
118:26	122
119:53	17
144	49
144:3–4	43
146	43–44, 49
146:3–4	43
146:7–8	43

Proverbs	20, 138
10:25	17
21:26	17
28	43, 49
28:1	17
28:16	42
29:6	17
29:16	17

Esther	
1:2	15

Ecclesiastes	4, 45, 47, 49
3	49
3:19	46
8	49
8:9	45
8:11–13	45
8:15	45
9	49
9:3	45–46
9:12–13	45
10:7	122

Isaiah	1, 11
20:4	23
22	23

40–55	2, 138	36:30	15
41:4–5	8	44:1	32
43:24–25	8	46:14	32
44:28	11	48:7	18
45	11	51:1	7
45:1	23	51:10	19
45:13	11	51:41	2, 7
45:25	17		
49	16		
49:1–5	15	**Ezekiel**	24, 42, 47, 122
51:12–13	44		
52	30–32, 41, 119	3:25	30
52–53	49	3:26	30
52:13	31, 56	16:15–16	44
52:13–15	2–3, 14, 28–29, 31–32	17:2–3	125
		24:18	40
52:13—53:12	31	24:26	30
52:14	28–29	27	16–17
52:15	29–30	27:12	16
53	3–4, 6, 28, 31–36, 38–39, 42–44, 46–49, 51–57, 118, 120, 123, 126, 132	27:33	16
		28:4	18
		34	2, 10–11
		34:18–19	10
53:2	35	40:1	24
53:3–7	117		
53:4–5	35–36	**Daniel**	13, 46–47
53:4–6	37		
53:5	57, 123	1:3–4	33
53:7	123	7	4, 46–47, 49–51, 53–55, 121, 132
53:8	35, 37–38, 123		
53:9	38, 124	7:13	134
53:10	4, 38, 40, 42–43, 45, 57	7:13–14	46, 53
		7:16	133
53:12	31, 35, 37, 123	9:24–27	118
54	8		
		Hosea	
Jeremiah			
		10:13	18
5:6	9	14:9	17
8:3	9		
13:16	9	**Amos**	
15:7	9		
19:1	22	4:2	18
29:22	18	5:20–21	19
36:11	13		

Micah

5:11	18
6:6–7	19

Habakkuk

2:4	17

Zechariah

9:9	122

Malachi

4:2	124
4:5	124

New Testament

Matthew	4, 51–52, 54, 121–22, 124–27
4:8	121
8:20	55, 133
9:6	132
9:15	122
10:23	132
11:19	55, 123, 132–33
12:8	52
12:32	133
12:40	133
13:37	133
13:41	133
13:41–42	53
16:13	133
16:27	132
17:9	132
17:12	55, 133
17:22	132
18:11	55, 133
19:28	132
20:18	132
20:28	133
24:27	52, 133
24:27–28	125
24:28	125
24:30	133
24:37	133
24:44	133
25:31	123, 133
26:2	133
26:24	132
26:45	133
26:54	120
26:56	120
27:29	121
27:52	124
27:57	124
27:60	124

Mark	4, 51–52, 54–57, 119–22, 124, 126–27
2:10	124, 132
2:10–11	1
2:28	52–53, 56, 132
8:29	122
8:31	52, 57, 127, 132
8:36	121
8:38	132
9:9	132
9:11	124
9:12	52, 54, 132
9:31	52, 57, 120, 132
10:33	52, 123, 132
10:33–34	58
10:38	123
10:45	54, 56, 125, 132
11:7	122
11:9	122
13:26	132
14:17–26	123
14:21	132
14:36	123

14:41	54, 132
14:47	123
14:48	123
14:49	57
14:62	121, 132
15:2–3	121
15:4–5	123
15:9–15	121
15:15	123
15:17	121
15:18	122
15:24	124
15:25	122
15:27	123
15:31	123
15:33	28, 124
15:43	124
16:1	124

Luke   4, 51–52, 54, 120–22, 126–27

4:18	123
5:24	132
6:5	52, 132
6:22	133
7:34	55, 133
9:22	57, 132
9:26	132
9:44	132
9:58	55, 133
11:30	133
12:8	133
12:10	133
12:40	133
17:22	133
17:24	52, 133
17:25	55, 133
17:26	133
17:30	133
18:8	133
18:31	132
19:10	55, 133
19:38	122
21:27	133
21:36	133
22:22	132
22:36–37	123
22:48	133
22:69	132
24:7	132
24:27	120
24:32	120
24:45–47	120

John   51–52, 54

1:51	134
3:13	134
3:14	134
5:27	134
6:27	134
6:53	134
6:62	134
8:28	134
12:23	53, 134
12:34	134
13:31	134

Acts

7:56	133

1 Corinthians

15:3–5	57

Hebrews

2:6	134

Revelation

14:14	134

Apocrypha and Septuagint

1 Esdras	50	Tobit	48
4:37	48	12:7	48
		12:11	48
1 Enoch	50		
		Wisdom	50
		9:4–7	48
Sirach	47, 50		
17:30–31	47		

www.ingramcontent.com/pod-product-compliance
Lightning Source LLC
Chambersburg PA
CBHW071508150426
43191CB00009B/1446